Escaping Leah

Ryan Prescott

escott

CONTENTS

WHY I WROTE THIS BOOK

For years you've been hearing certain criminals, con men, psychopaths, and the infamous bedsitters state they're "escaping" Scientology.

What does this even mean?

Well, it just means they were expelled and they're trying to use buzzwords to cover up their irresponsibilities and blatant crimes.

Let's be honest for a moment.

You've been getting the wrong information this entire time. Leah didn't escape the Church. The Church and its members escaped HER corruption, criminal behavior, and uninspiring self.

The purpose of this book is that one day some of these misinformed individuals can wake up and find that THEY can escape her grip, her web of lies, and her threats.

This is why I wrote this book. This is why it is necessary to share with others.

Thank you,
Ryan Prescott

FOREWORD

This book is presented here in official form and is part of a series exposing the crimes of those attacking new religious movements. This is a record of the author's research and discoveries through many means of internet, printed and verbal accounts.

The author may make claims that are offensive, straight forward, opinionated and otherwise matter of fact. These statements are not official statements of any Scientologist, any Church of Scientology, or any specific member of religious faiths.

This series is utterly based on research done from legitimate publications such as legal records that are of public record from around the world, statements made verbally or in writing, as well as direct personal encounters and knowledge.

Any information contained inside Escaping Leah is entirely non-fiction work and is backed by the Freedom of Speech as stated in the United Nations Universal Declaration of Human Rights and the US Constitution.

I believe that journalism shouldn't be attacked through verbal, legal or physical means. The author doesn't have any interest in surrendering to the attackers and stopping with his writings. The author will continue to express his thoughts as they are well within his rights.

We do hope that you have a better sense of understanding when reading this book.

"All truth passes through three stages.
First, it is ridiculed. Second, it is violently opposed.
Third, it is accepted as being self-evident."
- Arthur Schopenhauer

CHAPTER 1:
TROUBLEMAKER

L et's jump right into this by taking a chapter to hear from those who knew her, grew up with her, worked with her and tried to help. There's quite a lot that can be included here, but these passages share some highlights that let you see for yourself what she's made of, and these are their stories:

"What Leah is doing right now isn't so shocking to me. I actually started seeing some behaviors that I really kind of was like Whoa; this is not a nice person. And that hit me in 2008. We ended up becoming pretty close friends in the early 2000s. We, you know, she was at my baby shower in 2007. I was at her baby shower, birthdays, hanging out at her house, karaoke parties so we got to pretty close in I think 2000 to about 2007. Once she had her kid she definitely went into the 'I'm a new mom mode' and I didn't see her as much.

But it definitely hit me in 2008 at her sister's wedding. I was eight months pregnant and I was waddling in to go pee as very pregnant people do. And I opened the door to the lobby which is where we had entered and she looked right at me and said to somebody to her side 'I thought we closed this door to the public.' And I was like Oh! Oh, your friend, the 8-month pregnant person has to go pee and that's... that's where you're at. And I definitely, that was it for me. I was like 'Got it. I see where she's at now.'

And it definitely started I think when she became friends with Jennifer Lopez, like she definitely started becoming very self-important. There were so many times when...like one of our best friends sent out an email like 'Hey, let's go to Disneyland for my birthday.' And there's like 10 of us on the e-mail and they're all pretty—everyone knew each other and a pretty trusted group. And she had a real problem that she wasn't blind copied on it. It's like this is Disneyland we're talking about, like to your friends, and you want to be blind copied? So there's little clues that this, there were things that were not quite right. And her feeling very important, I think falsely.

You could always tell that there was a dark side that would sometimes pop up. She was constantly like digging for salaciousness or gossipy stuff. When you're joking around and it's lighthearted that fine but it's kind of like a little indicator that—you know that's where she lives. Like that's her little wheelhouse of, you know, what she likes to talk about. You know looking for dirt, always having you know the trash magazines around. And you know looking for stuff on other people or herself. I mean that's truly what I think Leah's doing here is trying to keep herself in the limelight. I mean that's really what I think this is about. Because I think her career started going downhill or you know the big show she was on, is no longer on and she needs money. And you know what bigger thing to give her money is sensationalism. And you know I think that's what this is. To a definite, a certain extent.

I believe she's even said if it wasn't for Scientology, who knows where she'd be, because she knows she has that darkness.

She's always been trying to control her inner beast. You know and she knows she can get nasty and mean and

Scientology was continually helping her to you know be a kinder nicer person, being happier with herself.

You know, the beast was too much for her. And you know with her career maybe you know, not being on a hit show, I don't know. She got fired from The Talk. Paychecks being of an issue. And her mom, who's, that's another subject, in her ear. It's like, "Hey, what better way than to make some money is to just try to attack Scientology."
- Julianne Williams, Former Friend

...

"When I really truly looked at Leah and her behavior, not only towards me but towards others, I realized that she was the biggest, baddest bully I've ever encountered in my life. She was ugly in the way she behaved to people and the way she treated people. Always trying to rip them apart. And it is just not somebody that you want to be around. That destructiveness was really awful. She's an awful being, an awful person. Awful ugly bully.

Leah was one of the chief sponsors of an event that I was producing. The stage was all set. The lighting was all done. The podium was in place and she came in, and Leah looked at the podium and she went, "I don't like that. Get rid of it. Put something else there." Without considering any of the production. It was just such a selfish move for her to do something like that. And this was a charity event.

Leah always had to be the center of attention in telling people what they should do and wanting to change something just on a whim that she felt she needed changed, instead of coming in and being kind about it and working with what we had. Because everybody else did that, but not Leah. She showed up and everything had to change just because of her.

As I got to know Leah more and more and I spent more time

with her on the set and other areas of her life, I saw that she was treating other people in that put down, condescending, actually very evil way. And I looked at that and I went I'm not going to work with somebody like that. I couldn't work with somebody like that who didn't appreciate others. I thought it was just me that she didn't appreciate, but then when I saw her with others it was true evil the way she was treating other people. And that's when I decided I couldn't work with her anymore, and didn't want to work with her because I didn't want to help somebody who was harming others all the time.

Always putting people down, always condescending, always treating them as if they weren't good enough for her, you know. And that's the way that she was treating me as well too.

It actually bothered me so much that I decided not to work with other actors as well, because I, wrongly, I thought maybe all other actors are like that. But one of the interesting things I found was that another young man that I was working with, he was at the beginning of his career as well too. When I told him I was going to stop managing, he couldn't have been kinder. And he said, ``You know, "Kathy you've worked so hard for me. You didn't get paid enough. I really didn't give you enough in return for everything"—me enough in return for everything that I did for him and he, if I ever needed help along the way he'd be more than happy to help me. And it was such a complete opposite of the way that Leah treated me. And treated others. I saw it all the time with her."
- Kathy Oliver, Former Manager

...

"Leah has always been vain and self-absorbed that I remember. It's pretty much always about Leah, and even with the family, she's that way.

So, I knew Leah when she was in her late teens and she definitely was the show, the comedian at all times. But she also was a comedian in a way that was like a put-down humor.

Well, that's Leah's whole acting ability, is basically her humor and making fun of others and their situations.

One time I was at one of her shows in the audience and a lady tripped and fell. And when Leah heard about it, she went, "Oh my gosh, that's hilarious I wish I could have seen it." The point is that humor was there but it's cruel. It's not a nice thing.

Leah attacked quite a bit when it was something where she felt uncomfortable or she felt it might have been her fault. Her way of thinking would be to attack.

And one time I was set up to come for an appointment to work with her child. When I got there they weren't there. So what I found out later, I said, "Where were you? We had an appointment." And she goes, "Wait a minute do you have an attitude with me?" And I'm going, "No I just was supposed to come and you weren't there and we had an appointment." And she goes, "I don't like this attitude that you're giving me." And I'm like "I'm not giving you an attitude." But I'm thinking, that's an interesting way to say it to someone who went out of their way to come and tutor your daughter.

Well, in Leah's household with her pretty much the boss, it was uncomfortable. It was uncomfortable for me but I'm not of that way. It's uncomfortable for her family and they used to fight with her but they didn't fight to the point where they felt better. I think they fought to the point where Leah pretty much was the aggressive one and they backed off. Because she was very aggressive and she was very, it was very well known that you don't talk like that to Leah. And if you do, it would be, you'd have to answer for it and it would be a problem for the person.

One time her sister said, "Well that's the wrath of Leah" and she was afraid of it. And it's just because Leah created a wrath about her. You know, and not a good way, a mean way and an aggressive way, which made you, think that she wasn't a very nice person.

Leah is pretty much playing a part. It's not really the way she is. She's not a victim at all. And she's not a big crusader for anything. What she is, is a crusader for herself."
- Connie Case, Former Family Friend

...

"My name is Jim Kilmartin and I have known Leah since she was a teenager. She initially hung around with one of my daughters. And later in life, my son ended up marrying Leah's sister.

When I used to go to Leah's house for the holidays, I never felt like I was part of the family. I mean my daughter was there. My son was there. So in that sense they were always happy to see me. But I never got that same feeling from Leah at all.

Leah never made me feel that I was part of the family. And when my wife, she was sick for quite a long time and in the hospital numerous times, I don't recall Leah ever coming to visit or calling me, or doing anything along those lines. You know, even know she talks about family, you know, I theoretically should have been part of the family considering my son's involvement, my daughter's involvement with Leah and the amount of time that went on for. And I don't remember her being at the memorial service. Or getting, when she passed away, or getting any kind of communication from her about my wife passing away. And so how is that caring about family?

Even though she says the family is very, very important, obviously I wasn't considered family. But yet I was.

I had gone to quite a few holiday events, whether it be Thanksgiving or Christmas or what not, at Leah's, and that was the most interaction I had, I guess you could

9

say, with her. And one time at one of these parties she wanted me to have something to eat. And I said "No I don't eat that kind of food." And for some reason that got her a little bit upset and from that moment forward I didn't get invited to as many things as I used to prior to that.

I would say the reason I didn't go back as much was because I didn't do what she wanted me to do and that didn't go over well."

- Jim Kilmartin, Former Father-in-Law of Leah's Sister

…

"So I think it was around five years ago Leah was here at the Church and staying at one of the buildings in a penthouse. And she called me to come over, she didn't like the furniture because it was dark wood and Leah likes everything white, which is fine. I have white furniture too. But Leah wanted everything removed, including the carpeting, and white furniture brought in. And I said, "Leah, this isn't your house you know. It's not the way I decorate either, but it's beautiful and it's nice and it's spotlessly clean." "No, can't live with this," so she had people go out and get her the furniture, in fact I went and got some for her; found her white furniture. And I found it a bit obsessive. I found it rude to the staff to make them do a job that they didn't really need to do.

Leah has never been an A-list celebrity, but she thinks she is. They don't demand all this extra attention. They're here like every one of the rest of us are here. But not Leah —she wants to be followed around and just given all this attention. I can remember saying to her at times, "Wow! How much attention do you really need?"

So she has everything redone. She has P-touches on all the drawers, the kitchen cabinets— champagne glasses, drinking glasses, white coffee cups. I remember saying, "Can't you just open the cabinet and see what there is there?"

I mean, she had to have it, you know, or open a drawer—white socks, black socks. On her desk, P-touched these plexiglass containers keys, pens. I just found it—like I say, I'm very organized, but I found that just a bit obsessive, okay? Like, "do you have nothing else to do with your time except P-touch? You can't see what's there?" I'm not being critical about it, I just found it a bit... I'm a designer myself and I design homes, but I've never gone to the extent of P-touching everything in somebody's house.

So she's staying in the penthouse and she doesn't like the food. She didn't like the dining room food and didn't want to go to the dining room. So she had a chef. And that doesn't come with the penthouse, you know what I mean? As far as I know, there's not a private chef that comes there and cooks for you. I guess you could request it, I don't know, I haven't stayed in the penthouse. But she has a private chef—she doesn't like the chef's cooking, so she orders a different chef to come and cook. I mean it was just—she was so demanding, that's the word, she was so—I've never met anybody as demanding as Leah was when she was here, to the point that it was embarrassing to me. It was really embarrassing and I would say, "Leah they're not your servants."

You know it doesn't matter in Scientology whether you make $10,000 a year, $100,000 a year or a million dollars a year, we're all on the same level. Nobody is treated according to how much money they make, where they come from and what they do. We all get treated the same. That's one of the beautiful things about the Church. But Leah doesn't kind of get it. Leah thinks that she needs to be treated like a total princess.

I never saw that Leah actually had any respect for anybody.

I guess that's a key thing. She didn't respect anyone, because it was just all about her. I mean not about anybody else, just all about Leah and nobody else.

And all I could think of, watching this, I kind of had to chuckle, is she's being an actress. And I sit there watching her interviewing these other people. And how Leah, with a tissue, and she's not really even crying. I mean, she's acting that she's crying or that she's so upset by what these people are saying.

On the show she says you have to do Scientology 365 days out of the year, minimum 2-1/2 hours a day. I never put in 2-1/2 hours a day. I never do Scientology 365 days a year. So she's lying on the show, she's having others lie on the show saying in order to do Scientology you have to do it 365 days a year. That's totally a lie. When I go and take a class, yeah it will be for a certain amount of time, a week, two weeks, maybe three weeks. But that certainly is not 365 days out of the year. Oh my god, how did I have three children? And how did I have three children, raised three children and have a life? She says you don't get to take vacations and you can't go anywhere, you can't do anything. That is an out-and-out lie. I take vacations; my friends take vacations, my daughter's off in Aspen right now skiing.

Leah, you talk about how we have to be here on course every day minimum 2-1/2 hours a day. When have you ever done that 365 days a year? When have you ever done that yourself, Leah?

So you've been lying the whole time, just like you're lying about a lot of things you're saying in your show. And what I want to know, that I want aired, is how much money are you making? I want to know how much money are you making to do this show and how much is Rinder and these other people that you have on the show? I'm sure they're all getting paid. I bet my bottom dollar they're all getting paid."
- Penny Jones, Former Friend

There's nothing to add to these stories. I know they're vetted, true and that they won't be silenced.

Leah is trying to bury her past; these experiences are only just the beginning.

CHAPTER 2: THE BUSINESS OF LEAH

If you thought Hitler was bad, wait until you hear about Remini. Their visions aren't too far apart and in fact, she is going for the extermination of Scientologists by making false accusations and inciting people to take violent actions actions based upon her lies.

A man with an arsenal of guns was arrested for threatening to assassinate the Church's ecclesiastical leader. Convicted of a felony and jailed, the man told police he was influenced by "the King of Queens lady."

Remini and her posse are looking at the total annihilation of a religion and their members due to their beliefs and practices that are assumed by those attacking it for reasons invented and for actions done by those who were attempting to infiltrate the religion and were caught.

A woman drove a car through the front doors of the Church of Scientology of Austin, Texas, stopping just short of the nursery. The convicted felon called Leah Remini "a true inspiration!!" and when informed that no one was hurt, her response was "That's too bad." The woman said "Thank you many times over to Leah Remini" as the inspiration for her crimes.

The first incident happened in Australia. A mid-twenty year old passed away after being brutally stabbed in his own Church while attending services. The last image that he saw was a teenager with a knife stabbing him to an unexpected death. Yes, it is hard to fathom but, it was inspired by Remini and her posse's content on A&E and their paid for stunts through the tabloids and the mainstream media.

And now, on January 3, 2019, a man fatally stabbed a member of our Australasian headquarters in Sydney. Previously the assailant had stated his intent to burn down the Church. The killer repeated the same lies and propaganda spread by Leah Remini and her co-host Mike Rinder on A&E's shows.

There are over 500 incidents of violent crimes, threats, harassment, and other such attempts that have just been brutally illegal.

Another social media follower of Leah Remini who comments on how she loves her show, tweeted: "I hope they burn down every building associated with Scientology."

Remini doesn't look at these as her doing and therefore will explain to her posse and her publicity people (Rinder and Ortega) that they aren't shedding light on this. She is denying it and deflecting.

Three days after the premiere of Remini's third season, an anonymous Twitter user named "Ben" posted a series of racist and violent threats including "We need shootings at every Scientology center."

The ideal scene of Remini is to have people yell with their right hand in the air, "Heil Remini". Sounds pretty extreme but, it's not.

She has opened the door to religious bigotry as well as complete discrimination, bullying, and harassment regarding Scientology's religious beliefs and practices. That is what you should look at in its entirety. There are children Scientologists in schools (private and public) that are experiencing all of the above. It is very sad.

Lies and deception are the only <u>actual</u> causes of this treatment. Hitler did this with the Jews. It was the cause of the concentration camps and the Nazis exterminating thousands of Jews. This was the end goal of the Nazis. Leah could definitely be looking in this direction, and if she's not, how much money is it worth to see people threatened and murdered?

We need to protect every religion and not just Scientology. No religion should be excluded from this. These are all fabulous groups of people with different beliefs and practices.

I'm unaware of what planet or country Remini thinks she lives in but, this is the United States of America and that's what the First Amendment covers. The Freedom of Religion is protected.

Freedom of Religion and Freedom of Speech were not meant to attack others for their beliefs and practices. That is what Hitler used to serve his twisted agenda of annihilating a whole religion and its members.

"Freedom of Speech does not mean freedom to harm by lies."
- L. Ron Hubbard, Scientology: A New Slant on Life

So, Remini, the sane will not be stating Heil Remini, the sane will be stating nothing of the sort. The insane who are your sheep will follow you until their last breath or until they finally wake up and wonder why the religion is still expanding and all these made up accusations are continuously disproved.

One day you, Remini, will end up where you never thought you would (or possibly were trying to avoid) which is your final destination, a fraudulent life, a life knowing that you have separated families, killed an innocent young man, had more than six hundred threats of violence and harassment on your former religion occur, contributed to your step-sister's passing, and the supporting of people from all sorts of criminal backgrounds.

CHAPTER 3: LIFETIME OF LYING

In Leah's mind she has millions of lawyers, attorneys, public relations representatives, and sane people that want to be her friend. This isn't reality. It's definitely sad.

It is clear that Leah Remini is living a fantasy which she unleashed after being expelled from Scientology. The officials who expelled her from Scientology made the correct call.

I do know <u>one</u> thing, Scientologists were <u>very</u> happy that she was expelled from the religion. They were constantly being used, harassed, slammed, and her errors in life would reflect on the religion. Being as though Scientology was never actually part of her life, she wasn't a representation for anything in Scientology.

So, based on these findings, it's all about one purpose that we cannot deny any longer...

> **"They [anti-Scientologists] view the Church as their 'lottery ticket' and pursue their jackpot with lies..."**
> — Mike Rinder

These allegations, misconceptions and false rumors have caused some viewpoints of "Scientology doesn't help," "Scientology isn't a religion," and "Leah was a Scientologist and it didn't help her."

In reality, the Church of Scientology is able to actually help people and Leah fights this thought on a daily basis and even tries to cover it up with tabloid pieces and also by throwing innocent family's traumatic experiences into the air and blaming it on the Scientology religion for profit and attention. Thus, Scientology is thought of by the insane as anything but a religion based on these fallacies that she's pushed off on people.

As I've stated previously, Remini was never a Scientologist. It is incorrect to assume Scientology had anything to do with Leah's downfall. Scientologists tried to assist Leah, she wouldn't accept any help, hence she just kept failing.

I do want to make one thing clear, Scientology does help people and has ever since its conception in 1952. Scientologists have acknowledged Scientology for its help in their lives.

> **"Before I became a Scientologist, I thought that I would come out of school, I would get a job and have this job for 40 years and then retire, I just wanted a simple job, not much stress, just a stable job. I just wanted stability. Since I became a Scientologist, I ended up changing careers, which I was able to do because I was encouraged to follow my dreams. Scientology means solutions to every single aspect of life. It's the technology of life."**
> - Niki, Real Estate Agent

The cold-hard fact of Leah Remini is that she wasn't a Scientologist. If she were, she wouldn't have any problems following the ethical standards, continuing on the services of the Church and so many other aspects, including the privacy of the lives of others.

It is based on the fact that she wasn't ever a Scientologist that I speak out against her. Leah's viewpoint doesn't matter as she used Scientology as a prop and Scientologists for her connections to boost her ego and as an attempt to reach her dreams of becoming a successful actress.

I'm stating through my own research that Leah is lying to those who are gullible and those who may not have the ability to get the right data. I believe that in an ethical society Leah's actions would be frowned upon but, today's society is all about the ratings, buzzwords and money.

She denies <u>all</u> responsibility in regards to her unethical conduct in Scientology. I did a study regarding the ethical conduct of Scientologists and here is what I found them stating:

"The ethics and justice codes of Scientology are actually very pure in their form. They keep me on track for success and don't let me get distracted by unethical conduct like, cheating, taking drugs, and being unproductive in life and having people pay for my absence in society." - F.S.

"Living in a society that is completely and utterly falling on its face through political divides, pornography, rape, human trafficking, and other forms of completely raunchy behavior, is quite difficult. It is very easy to become unethical in this society as it is no longer looked down on in society. Using what LRH laid out for ethics is completely necessary for me to be successful in this day and age." - A.D.

"Being a principal in a school full of youngsters that have dreams and goals of becoming something big and then having the influence that society is giving them of complete UN-productiveness, lack of morals, and just freely doing what is clearly illegal – it is a challenge. I use Scientology to keep my life in the boundaries of ethical conduct and thus help others use my life as an example." - P.M.

These ethical standards aren't hard to follow. I know <u>many</u> men and women who follow these and are excelling in their lives. Leah must think being ethical is boring and unlike her. She has talked about her "status" (gloating about her huge ego) as if it was something high and mighty, which was completely the opposite of reality.

> **"I was acting in an episode of *King of Queens*. I was cast in it. I didn't know Leah or anybody in her family beforehand. I just was cast and when I arrived on the set for rehearsal that week, immediately she'd had a huge blow up with the director, and she was acting very mean and pretty awful. And they actually had to shut the set down for at least an hour while she, you know, whatever, cooled off, came back. And then, and she was pretty mean the whole week. And because I knew she was a Scientologist I actually was embarrassed that she was acting that way."**
> - Shannon B., Actress

Scientologists are treated equally and <u>regardless</u> of their contributions and actions in Scientology. They may be respected for what they've done and even acknowledged.

No, Leah did not get many people into the religion. She didn't donate millions of dollars and she wasn't asked to. She was told to get her career off of the ground for her own good, that's all. Her life was organized to a certain degree but, she was still trying to find her way in becoming a respected, well-known and successful actress.

Leah wasn't a participant in Scientology. She wasn't valued above any other Scientologist. She really had no <u>actual</u> relationship with the Scientologists in the entertainment industry because she'd use them and then burn the relationship.

You'd never find Leah at a fundraising event donating for the good of the cause, she'd donate for the publicity of doing a respectable contribution. She never valued the purpose of fundraising. If Leah did, she'd be a Scientologist today because that purpose would be to better society through humanitarian initiatives that are wholly non-religious.

Kirstie Alley for instance fights for the rights of children and the elderly from being electro-shocked and drugged against their will. She does this in partnership with the Citizens Commission on Human Rights (Scientologists support this watchdog group on Psychiatric abuses and violations). Kirstie and her beautiful family have been doing this since it was started.

Tom Cruise is not treated like royalty in the Church. Tom doesn't need special treatment and doesn't do things for attention. He has spent his years fulfilling his goals and improving himself through the use of Scientology principles. He has also contributed time, funds, and other forms of help towards the religion and its supported humanitarian initiatives.

Leah has used Scientologists' names in the media to spark some attention for herself, to boost her ego, and most of all – rake in the money. She has no care in the world for them, she only cares about the work orders from her masters.

So, the totality of Leah's statements are based on no evidence, no personal experience, no encounters, and no understanding of Scientology or Scientologists.

Lies have no basis in truth. Lies can be repeated over and over again but, it doesn't make them true.

CHAPTER 4:
AFTERMATH OF
THE AFTERMATH

L eah's posse is actually geared towards making a group that generates money through creating bad propaganda about religion. In fact, even though they pretend to 'expose' all religions, Scientology is the only real religion that they care about attacking and all the others are just publicity cover-ups.

Those supporting this are people like retired bitter people, Psychiatrists and Psychologists, brainwashers, deprogrammers, kidnappers, criminals, rapists, and other investors. These investors are people who have contributed time or money toward the purpose of attacking Scientology for profit and an attempt at some "true" fame.

Leah is not successful at this alone. She needs people that she can make work for her and pay them through her swindles and her defamation. This is actually easily laid out.

Why would someone want to attack Scientology? Why would someone want to attack any religion for that matter? It is not always because of the fact that there is some "illegal activity" or some other buzzword – it is because the religion is making people better and more aware! That is actually it! It's helping people and that's a BIG problem for some folks out there.

This is a conversation with Mark Rathbun (Leah's Former Guru) and Leah Remini:

> **Marty Rathbun: "I'm really impressed how you guys had the courage to do that and share that with people. I mean that's pretty personal right there. I got one problem with it though, I mean I think it was really terrible how you just dumped it all on your mother and made her look like she was the villain of the piece and somehow unintelligent and stupid, bi, and culpable."**

> **Leah Remini: "No no no, you didn't get it at all, this wasn't an actual therapy session, this whole thing was planned and scripted."**

> **Marty Rathbun: "You literally acted?"**

> **Leah Remini: "Yeah, we literally, just listen that's how it works honey doll. That's how you do it. It's not reality, I work out I plan out all these episodes and we figure them out beforehand. Who's going to say what, who's going to do what. What do you think I was going to put a camera on myself?"**

Leah Remini confessed to scripting a therapy session. She did this for the ratings and not for the "heroic" value that she tries to display through her production.

This is what Leah Remini said on ABC 20/20 about what she is doing:

> **"I don't work for free. This is a very demanding job. I mean, I'm just a crappy has-been actress who is trying to make a dollar off my Church. What do you think about that, Dan?**
> **"You're an asshole."**
> - Leah Remini, 2017

You should also look at the interview with *The Hollywood Reporter:*

> **"THR: Leah, I want to turn to you... How much vetting is done of the people who are going to tell their stories on your show? Is that something...? Do you have people who have to sort of make them prove their stories?**
>
> **Leah Remini: What... What do you want me to do? 'Prove it to me?' You know? So there is NO VETTING I go take their word for it.**
>
> **THR: And Legal will let you get away with that?**
>
> **Leah Remini: Well they have to. Because they are 'my people'. "**

Leah Remini isn't interested in the truth, she wants the ratings, the popularity, and the cash flow that comes with scamming.

The obvious point is Leah doesn't vet those she talks to about their "experiences" in Scientology. As you can already assume, they're scripted or invented for a few moments of fame.

These people come from the depths of the worst industries to the most corrupt organizations. It is actually quite eye-opening the amount of people who band together for a criminal mission.

> **"Individuals with criminal minds tend to band together since the presence of other criminals about them tends to prove their own distorted ideas of man in general."**
> —L. Ron Hubbard

Leah and her posse make it seem like what happened in the past (by key people in her posse who were pretending to be Scientologists) is happening today. But, in fact, Scientology has corrected every past incident that occurred and has made the past preventable.

Additionally, David Miscavige has also released key information on the past incidents so that officials of the church today can make sure that when people see those "symptoms" they can do something to stop what could happen next, using L. Ron Hubbard's policies and the laws of the land.

People like Leah Remini and her posse will not make it an inch into the religion's churches with these safe guards in place. It's been very effective and has prevented some of the largest and gnarly attacks on the Church of Scientology.

I remember talking to an official of the Church and I remember asking this official **"Did Leah Remini actually mean anything to Scientology?"** and the official replied with:

"Leah Remini really didn't mean anything to Scientology. She claims that she did so much for the religion but, in fact, all she did was revolve around gossip, throw tantrums, and give here and there when people really needed it. That was actually stretching her pocket because she really didn't have a job."

Leah has claimed that she's pissed off individuals in Scientology for telling the truth about it. If this were the case, Scientology would actually be settling the situation with Leah and her posse, therefore it isn't the case.

I would urge her to wake up from the fantasies. She needs to smell the cow dung and get on with the reality of her decisions and where her unethical conduct led her.

The one thing I would thank this gnarly production for is weeding out the insane and the very evil individuals. The lies have cleared out these individuals from ever coming onto a Scientologist's radar of help. Scientologists no longer have to waste their time with those who would rather live an unsuccessful, unethical, and dangerous life.

The Church of Scientology has shown through all of the decisions it made to expel these individuals that it was the right thing to do. The Church is now expanding more than ever and Scientologists are happier because of these apostates being moved off the lines.

CHAPTER 5:
UNLIKELY PAIRING

Leah has made many positive statements about Scientology and they don't seem to reach the light of day. This is intentional as Leah would rather not share this side of the story. The positive parts of Scientology never seem to reach the press.

These statements are completely voluntary and in the midst of her operations as a pretending Scientologist and in the process of using Scientologists who are in the entertainment industry to attempt to better her career and her actress profile.

Here are public interviews that Leah did voluntarily to share her successes and her experiences with Scientology. These interviews were done with stations like the BBC and were also done at the Church's community events to have those in attendance share their thoughts.

> "I didn't really have any involvement [with the community] prior to getting involved with Scientology in any way, it was just kind of like, 'ME, ME, ME!' you know? It's like, 'I'm screwed up, I need help, and screw everybody else!' And since I've been involved in Scientology you know you learn to take responsibility for yourself and not only yourself but others and so the focus gets a little bit off of you and that's always a

good thing. You know and that it's not all about Leah and my problems and my garbage. And it feels good to know that you can actually make a change because people can, people can make a difference."
- Leah Remini, 1997

Leah seems to be displaying how much Scientology has assisted her thus far in taking responsibility for her life and the lives of others.

Scientology does offer various services for this particular aspect in life. She may be referring to receiving spiritual counseling or taking a few courses on the subject of responsibility.

This doesn't seem to pretend as if this statement would "go away" the next day nor the next year. This seems like a life-changing success. This shows some serious results.

What happened to the above? Why hasn't she taken any responsibility for her violations in Scientology?

It seems to me that her ability to take responsibility for herself and others faded away. Could it be that she decided not to take responsibility and to blame others for her own decisions?

"It's nice to know when you do something and you go, 'I'm actually helping,' you know, I'm helping them help. I'm helping the Church help so many other things and that's such a—I love it, I love being involved with it, because then I, you know, I feel like I'm a good person." - *Leah Remini, 1997*

Leah looks to be finding helping to be a good thing and in return, she is happy about it. She also openly admits that she's helping the Church <u>help</u> people.

The Church has "so many other things" going on every single day of the year. The Church helps 365 days a year with criminal reform, character building, drug prevention and rehabilitation, human rights awareness and much more.

I wouldn't doubt that she was inspired enough to want to help the Church with helping others. She must've known that it was a worthwhile cause otherwise she wouldn't have done anything.

"I don't know of an organization that has their hands in so many things in the community, especially when it has to do with children and the environment, and that's a beautiful thing. Yeah, so they give so much, I mean it's crazy.

Well, I'm an artist, so like I said, without it I'd be in the dumps and I would probably be an animal, I would be a horrible, horrible person."
- Leah Remini, 1998

This was a statement made a year after the earlier ones outlining responsibility, helping others, and having her attention from herself all the time.

Leah went from helping Scientology help others to understanding that Scientology has their hands in so many things in communities. What really touched her the most was the children being helped. She must've been able to experience helping the children with their studies, human rights education, character building, and even making them smile.

She actually <u>saw</u> how crazy it is that Scientology gives so much. I even think it's crazy how much the Church does for communities around the world. From my experience, the Church has helped so much that my friends (who aren't religious) have noticed a difference in areas where Scientology has assisted.

Do you know what's special about the above statement she made? She told you that <u>without</u> Scientology she'd be a horrible person and that she'd be an animal. This means that something made her feel this way.

Leah may act stupid on the screen and she may be a drama queen but, she knows Scientology helps individuals. She is not dumb. She must've been swindled into some type of deal with *very* bad individuals and judging by her career, she couldn't refuse it.

"Celebrity Center is my second home and there is not a person here that I can't go to when I am having a problem in my life, or I'm, you know, things are not going well, there is something here for everybody."
- Leah Remini, 1999

Two years after Leah found out that Scientology helps people, that she can take responsibility, and that communities are bettering because of Scientology, she finds an official Church to call home.

Leah made it to the Celebrity Center and Church of Scientology in Los Angeles, California. She found this Church to be her second home. She felt safe at this Church. I don't blame her, this Church location is beautiful and the staff are delightful.

From my sources, she was involved in many community programs and she was doing them through the Celebrity Center and Church of Scientology in Los Angeles. She was helping in these programs constantly and working with some of the committed staff of the Church (as they were the executives in-charge of the overall humanitarian initiative).

"Without any Scientology organization things are not going to change on this planet. We are the most ethical group you are ever going to find, and actually the only group that's really making change for mankind."
- Leah Remini, 1999

Leah helped with humanitarian initiatives in most of 1999. She was doing a great job working with Scientologists attending Church services and helping spread the word about special projects and future plans of the humanitarian initiatives and their distribution around Los Angeles.

It looks like Leah found out for herself something about Scientology. She must've done some digging to see what other Scientologists were up to around the community and based on her previous statements, it looks like she found that Scientology is the most ethical group on the planet.

There is something you didn't catch in the statement. Leah says "we" are the most ethical group you are ever going to find. She is, of course, referring to Scientologists and she has put herself into that same group.

"I could go on forever about Celebrity Center, but really if I just have to say in layman terms what it is for me, is it's like having a best friend for life, it's like the best friend who is always home, the best friend who doesn't have a problem, the best friend who is always there for you regardless and that's what CC has been for me and my family is pure friend, regardless of what is going on in the world CC has always been here for me as a friend and I cherish it, I really—it's one of the gifts that's been given to me as an artist."
- Leah Remini, 2000

Leah has already stated that Scientologists are the most ethical group you are ever going to find on this planet. She has already confessed that the Church of Scientology and Celebrity Center in Los Angeles is her second home.

She is now stating that this Church is like having a best friend for life, who's always home, doesn't have a problem, always there for you regardless, and how it's been a pure friend to her family.

This Church location and their staff is one of the gifts that has been given to her as an artist. This is completely special and shouldn't be slandered or attacked.

After reading this statement, I wonder if any outsider who has hate for the Church actually attacked her on this statement. I'm thinking analytically, why else would she leave the Church after saying this? In my mind, this doesn't just fade away, this type of statement stays with you <u>forever</u>.

"I don't get along with others and there is so many things that Scientology has helped me with I don't think I would be ME really without Scientology I don't think I'd have the success that I have without Scientology I wouldn't be the girlfriend that I am, the daughter that I am, the sister that I am, because this is all because of Scientology and what Scientology has taught me."
- Leah Remini, 2001

Leah has already stated a lot of interestingly positive statements about Scientology. These are all very personal and very enlightening.

She confesses here that she doesn't get along well with others. I don't think many of us starting out get along with others. That's just the truth of the matter. Scientology has courses for this because it's a common area people would like help with. There are many other courses on communication, relationships, and other aspects that could help improve this <u>one</u> aspect of anyone's life. It won't take thousands of dollars, a risk of failure, or a magical potion.

Leah states that she wouldn't be her without Scientology. She stated this in another way previously stating that she'd be an animal and a horrible person. She basically solidified her point that Scientology is helping her improve on many aspects of her life.

"I think as an artist you get a lot of crap on a daily basis. You need something, it's either going to be drugs or something positive. And Scientology is positive. So I think that's why people are drawn to it, that's the bottom line."
- Leah Remini, 2001

She makes a good point here, artists do get a lot of crap on a daily basis. You don't need a degree to see this fact. A glimpse of the recent news cycle can clue you in.

The next point that Leah makes is that artists need something and they either turn to drugs or something positive. She claims Scientology is positive.

Leah believes people are drawn to Scientology because it's positive. That's the bottom line of it all. It isn't the flashy ads, the prominent members, and it isn't about any other aspect. It's completely true it's positive and that is genuinely why a majority are drawn to it.

"What Scientology has helped me with is confidence. I've had somewhere to go to tell someone my fears and I wasn't crazy, you know, that I could actually do something about those fears, that I could actually be in control of my own feelings, that I could actually be in control of my own career, and that's what Scientology has helped me with. And I think it's important for an artist to have some outlet other than your mom who is like "Ah, just shut up and go on another audition," You know, you need some other help and it's offered me that help."
- Leah Remini, 2002

Apparently, Scientology helped Leah Remini with her confidence, and that is a welcome improvement for anyone, especially an artist. Instead of being judged by others for her problems in life, she's trusted the Church of Scientology to help her and be her sounding board. She's been able to improve her life from this aspect.

She made a lot of good points in this statement. There's one point that I think really matters the most to her and that's her mom's viewpoint of "just shut up and go on another audition". Basically toughening it up and moving on. This isn't healthy for anyone.

"With Scientology I was able to have success in this business without compromising my own integrity. And that's what Scientology helped affirm for me."
- Leah Remini, 2002

Apparently, Leah actually used Scientology principles to have success in the entertainment industry and have success without invalidating her personal integrity.

This is actually a great improvement to have. You cannot get this from many places. Tom Cruise, Chick Corea, and Giovanni Ribisi (to name a few) have used Scientology principles as well and look where they are today.

"I didn't want to follow the crowd of people, like the bad people but I also wanted to be a cool person so I was like kind of struggling with the two personalities but being a Scientologist you're getting in touch with the person that you really are and we really are good people... so I've avoided all that by being a Scientologist and by having integrity and by living by certain moral codes that this group abides by, I can look at myself in the mirror ..."
- Leah Remini, 2003

She mentions that she's avoided "all that" by having integrity and by living by certain moral codes that this group abides by and that she can look at herself in the mirror. This is a lot to say to be shattered 13 years later, slamming the ethical codes of Scientology as "hard to follow".

There is a point in this statement where she says that she's avoiding the bad people by being a Scientologist. Could it be that she was still struggling with this ten years later?

"Celebrity Center has made a big difference in my life because as I really feel this is a home away from home. Like I—you know, you don't find that in many places in your lifetime. And it's a special place because whatever you're going through

there's somebody always here to help you. It's like having your best friend who has all the answers, the right answers!

Celebrity Center inspires me to try to help where I can, and do things that I could do that might make some positive change."
- Leah Remini, 2003

It's clear that Leah Remini believes this Church has made a huge difference in her life and that she believes that it's her home. It's her home because she is always able to get help and answers. She emphasizes that it's not just answers but, <u>right</u> answers.

She has also brought attention to the Church for inspiring her to help wherever she can to bring some positive change to the community. This is a great thing.

What the hell happened?

"Because I am Scientologist I know what we do for the community, but when we have political leaders coming and mayors of other cities coming and umh... People in law enforcement coming and praising what we do and how we are helping the community, it just, it warms my heart to hear these stories and I hope other people share in that. I wish this would air everywhere you know? I wish this would air on network television."
- Leah Remini, 2006

In this interview she was at her favorite Church at one of their community gatherings. Leah mentions that because she's a Scientologist (or at least puts herself in that category), she's aware of what Scientology does for the community. This is also the area of her involvement for the past couple of years of statements.

She even goes so far as to state that she loves when officials and representatives stop by and praise what Scientology is doing and to find out how Scientology is helping their community.

I don't know if Leah Remini knows this, but Scientology ten years later has a TV channel where these are being aired everywhere around the world on social platforms and DirecTV channel 320.

> **"And I have included myself in this category of, you know, this makes me legit, you know, if I have a house that looks like this and a car that looks like that or boobs that look like this then I'm legit, you know, I am really in this business and I am really someone to be reckoned with. And you know, I've gone down that path, I don't really have the boobs but I have the other things and it's an empty happiness and I see it time and time again. I have successful friends in all areas of the entertainment industry and what I see are failed marriages, failed relationships, unhappiness, depression is a big one. I am not a depressed person. And I guess I take it for granted because I've been in Scientology most of my life but that's what I see, I see these are definite traps that you have to look this way and act this way as opposed to really being a well-adjusted, happy human being with integrity."**
> - Leah Remini, 2006

Leah makes a valid point here. There are <u>major</u> situations people in the entertainment industry are going through. These aren't to be ignored. When you are looking at prominent celebrities you see "perfection," "flawlessness," and many other aspects that companies push onto you.

The point about this statement she made is that Scientology makes her aware of these traps. These are mental and physical traps that aren't full of any happiness.

> **"Inglewood org is the first of its kind in that it is truly for the community; it's what LRH would want. And to be able to see his dream lived out in such a big way just touches my heart. Because it really is the first of its kind, this org."**
> - Leah Remini, 2011

Leah attended the grand opening for the Church of Scientology and Community Center of Inglewood, California. You can see that she was looking at this opening through the bigger picture of what this will do for the future of society and for the vision of L. Ron Hubbard.

This 'Ideal Org' really touched her heart. This is completely understandable as she'd been involving herself in the community outreach out the Church of Scientology for over 10 years at this point.

She also by this point understood why it was <u>extremely</u> important to open 'Ideal Orgs' everywhere to fulfill the demand for Scientology and to help communities with the outreach of the Church of Scientology's supported humanitarian initiatives.

"It makes me feel whole, there is a piece of me now that was missing and when I had the idea to start a mission here. It really came out of having been raised in a community that was diverse. And when you move to California, you don't really have that neighborhood feeling. I didn't even know my neighbors until there was an earthquake. And the only reason you know them then, is because they feel an obligation to knock on your door and go, "Are you okay?" reluctantly. But I didn't grow up that way. I grew up in a community like this. So for me this is a piece of my heart."
- Leah Remini, 2011

Wow, this statement went from just helping in the community to fully contributing to the Scientology movement by wanting to open a smaller sized Church of Scientology.

She was truly touched by the opening of the Church of Scientology and Community Center in Inglewood, California. She recalled wanting to help uplift the community.

Leah shared a piece of her mindset, at this grand opening, through this statement. She detailed the importance of responsibility, care, and neighborhoods. It's a diverse group of individuals that live in the same area and are for the same purpose – to survive.

> **"This org represents actually getting out in the community, and dealing one on one with an individual. It's about taking somebody who is on drugs, who is maybe walking off the street, going 'What is this Community Center?' 'What is this org?' 'What is this Church?' Walking in and going: 'We can help you. You want to learn how to read? Sit down.' I mean, to be able to connect our Church with LRH's life betterment programs—it's just never been done. So for me, this is what it's about."**
> - Leah Remini, 2011

For Leah the Inglewood Scientology organization was a blessing for her. Truly, she has had three part interviews on this organization and what it is doing for the community and the fact that L. Ron Hubbard's principles and social betterment programs are there to help the community means a lot to her.

Leah lays out the exact process to getting help from the Church of Scientology. There are no other steps or qualifications, you just need to *want* to be helped. The Church will assist you with the main aspects of life and be there as your friend through thick and thin.

I think Leah knew deep down inside, when she was expelled, that she lost the one group that cared enough to help her (as she admits). I can only assume that she was bought out by the attackers of the Church and she took it as an easy way to make income besides doing it through hard work.

Here is an interview with BBC reporter, John Sweeney,

> **"Let's take us for example. We are best friends, and I am a Scientologist and you are not. That's great. You know, I'm going to be your friend regardless. I want the best for you;**

you want the best for me. You start every day talking about something that I believe in and you start being disrespectful to my religion, to me you've crossed the line. But that's on any religion. I wouldn't be disrespectful to any of my friends' religion. Or think that they should put up with that. It's just disrespectful."
- Leah Remini, 2007

Based on this statement she's stating that if you're disrespectful to her religion, you've crossed the line. She won't respect you after that. This isn't just on her religion but, <u>any</u> religion.

Why after this statement does she then attack Scientology? There has to be a catch that we're missing. She must've spoke with an attacker and got a substantial bribe.

Or, how about the one where she criticizes the Scientology attackers in the same interview with BBC:

"I've met a lot of people who were ex-Scientologists. They usually don't, they usually don't say anything to me. Just as I wouldn't say anything about their religion, or whatever they are doing. You know, I wish them the best. You know, I want them to live a good life. I'm not going to sit and name call and—you know if it's not for you it's not for you! You know what I mean? I'm not going to go off—if I go get a bad facial am I going to spend the rest of the day going, you know, "This salon over here isn't…" you know? I mean it's just like, it's just a waste of time. Just go on with your life. I get scared of people who run around making this their, their like mission in life. It's like, please. It's, it's crazy, but it's insane. There's so many things to be doing in life rather than running after people who are doing good!

"And you don't have to be a Scientologist. I could care less if you are a Scientologist. But I care about you as a human being."
- Leah Remini, 2007

She's actually telling you in this statement that if she had a bad facial, she wouldn't go around spreading it. She would simply say it wasn't for me and it wasn't for you.

I wish that was what was happening today, she is going around stating some horrendous things about Scientology. As far as these statements go, there seems to have been nothing wrong with Scientology's services, involvement, and staff.

She defends the Church in this statement to BBC reporter, John Sweeney. This was uncalled for at the time and she volunteered to help combat John's attacks at Scientology.

I hope these are as eye-opening to you as they are to me.

CHAPTER 6: LEAH
IS A LIAR

L eah is good at upsetting people and creating drama and conflict using the tried and true false accusations of earlier apostates. Yes, all her claims are not actually hers. They are recycled lines from many years ago. This leads to the simple truth that she's a liar and the facts are easy to prove simply by going through different court documents that lay out all the false accusations made against the Church for the past three decades.

What I run into are people who have been misled and become emotionally upset about the tragic claims. People who watch Leah's TV series of nothingness actually start to go crazy due to the fact that it confuses them utterly. This is how I helped people escape Leah's thinking.

I have had many people reach out to me as a Scientologist and they ask me questions about what Leah's big mouth spewed out. I laugh and then answer the question. It is very simple. The information she gives isn't real and the facts are completely false, so it is very easy to tell them what the truth is and it normally calms them down and gets them focused on reality. Later in the book you can see specific evidence to confirm my statements so this is not just opinion.

I was at a disaster site in Jacksonville, North Carolina, when a man came up to our Volunteer Ministers tent asking for supplies, food, and refreshments and as we handed him all of it he asked us a question. I was shocked that he had heard anything of Scientology as we were in a state that didn't have a prominent location quite yet.

He asked "Do you really believe in taking people away from their families?" and I replied with "Ha! You must've heard this from Leah, right?" and he said "Yes, in fact, I was quite appalled at it all." and I said "I bet, she uses buzzwords, soundbites, and invented claims to try to fill her pockets and make her more popular. We don't take people away from their families. I am with my family and people who I know who're with other religions and their family members are Scientologists are still family and they hang out all of the time." He replied with "I knew it was a pile of shit from the beginning of her series. I kept telling my wife and then she made me give her a chance, we won't be watching her again. Thank you guys for what you're doing here for us all."

That is just one instance out of many that have asked a question about Scientology and what they've heard and immediately made up their own mind based on the **truth**. That is the example of thinking for yourself based on the truth. It only takes a little effort to do some background checking, and if you've had trouble with this in the past, well that's why I'm writing these books.

During Hurricane Florence it was a complete honor to help those affected and I want to say that I was not there to promote my religious beliefs, but merely to show that Scientology is here to help them even in their darkest time. We don't want anything in return but a smiling face and to know that we helped!

Thinking in terms of Leah is to think in terms of being unsuccessful and a complete bigot. Being Leah Remini doesn't actually require any such skill that you would need to acquire from education, of any form, but actually just selling other peoples' lies and filming yourself stating the lies and working with infiltrators and corrupt people to be acknowledged for the lies.

Basically, she works with those who don't care if they work tomorrow as long as they are known today for something that Leah states as "heroic". And, to think this was all because she was declined $1.5 million dollars of extortion money from the Church for whatever her false claims were.

Leah thinks in terms of herself and what is going to benefit her and that's it. There is no such thing as someone else in her mind. Her posse all fend for themselves and when she gets paid, they probably have to convince her to actually pay them their cut.

She turns everything Scientology does well into something that is dangerous for some insane reason. It is actually quite crazy how her thought process turns out. Scientology hasn't done anything crazy compared to other religions and organizations. She will make up some crazy stories.

In fact, one of Leah's "side gigs" is convincing others to file lawsuits against the church in an attempt to try to take it down. It doesn't matter if they get dismissed and thrown out of court later. The bad press which circulates with the news of the suit being filed is exactly how she fuels her scam.

The suits are usually geared toward attacking Scientology and their officials for things that they haven't actually done and would never do. Where do they get the information that they put in the lawsuits? They put their own wrongdoings that they committed in the Church and those things got them expelled and almost arrested.

The lawsuits against Scientology are geared towards trying to damage a reputation.

Here is what Leah's right-hand man had to say about it:

"The sheer volume of despicable allegations made about him are intended to create the false impression that where there is smoke there is fire. These "witnesses" know only too well from their experience in the Church that the tactic of telling bigger and bolder lies has been a strategy employed against the Church in litigation for years.

"Tell enough lies, and make enough allegations, and an impression will be created which accomplishes the end of destroying a reputation no matter how untrue the allegations are. Public figures are especially susceptible to this fraud as any study of history shows.
Jesus Christ was crucified based on the false accusations of Judas Iscariot and the prejudice of the Romans."
- Mike Rinder, Testimony in 1994

Being as though the above statement was made under penalty of perjury in the US of A, this should be taken with higher authority than all of the other statements this posse has made.

In 1994, Mike Rinder (Leah's side man) was employed in the Church of Scientology International as the Scientology Spokesperson. He was entrusted with honestly representing Scientology and Scientologists in the press, news, media, and even in the courts. He did just that and this wasn't an altered statement.

Mike Rinder stated this in a testimony that was done in 1994 that was regarding some allegations against Mr. David Miscavige, the leader of Scientology religion. These court cases, just like all of the others, were thrown out as being baseless. That is the truth of the matter.

The posse will claim that Mike was paid to state this. Well, the Spokesperson is supposed to be honest and truthful and correctly report under oath what is occurring. If something is occurring and you're under oath, you need to state it or otherwise handle it with the opposing party and/or the judge. You would have to be straight and honest with people and you would take responsibility for what did occur that was wrong. It's illegal to lie in this way.

Leah thinks that eventually the Church will cave in and pay all of their members' donations and such for some baseless claim and her publicity stunts. That won't happen. She is not their problem anymore; she is not a Scientologist and she was expelled. Scientologists are happy that she is not in the religion after everything that she has done with her life and how she sold her soul to the tabloids and the buzzword companies. If the Church of Scientology had someone like this in the religion, this person would be the craziest member ever and *that* is what would go all over the news and nothing about what this crazy person was saying would ever catch any light.

You can continue to defend her thinking and in fact, you should buy a Bible of hers. She should definitely decide to write a Bible for all of the sheep that follow her and her supporters because she surely is making ends meet on whatever she is doing with religious bigotry and playing the media by puppet strings.

The only thing I can really look at about her is the fact that she is evilly smart but that only lasts for a little while and then it starts to bite her in the ass. It really starts to hurt her. She is emotionless so it wouldn't matter anyway; she has lost too many jobs and possessions to care.

My advice and/or suggestion would be to _not_ follow her path in life because it doesn't end well. It may look good from a far but, in actuality, she is going to have to fess up to what she has stated that is contrary to the actual facts of the religion.

Why would you listen to me? Well, being as though I have been a Scientologist and my accomplishments inside and outside the religion are quite good for people my age, I would have some good knowledge to share with people.

Just make a point to look at some facts and don't take my word or hers. Would she ever tell you to look at the facts? Probably just the 'facts' she presents...

CHAPTER 7: LEAH'S OBSESSION WITH DAVID MISCAVIGE

David Miscavige is the Leader of the Scientology Religion. He is known as the Leader and as the Chairman, not as a god or anything different from you and me. However since the day that Leah conceived the thought that Scientology has a Leader, it seems that she fell secretly in love with him.

Here are some examples to fit this "conspiracy" if you'd like to call it that...

1. Before being expelled, she requested that she be the adviser for David Miscavige. She was declined. She wouldn't take this for an answer.

2. After her attempts to get close to Mr. Miscavige she turned very bitter. For example, while at Tom Cruise and Katie Holmes' wedding, she got drunk and the first thing she did was yell obscenities in the direction of Mr. Miscavige.

3. Probably most obvious is how Leah has been in a crazed rage about harassing Mr. Miscavige's wife. David's wife wants nothing to do with Leah or any of her posse. Leah has been telling

people she's missing, simply because his wife prefers privacy and not to be in the spotlight of the media.

These are a few examples to support why I came up with the conspiracy theory. Hell hath no fury as that of a scorned woman.

Leah has attempted to attack anyone that has affiliation with Mr. Miscavige because she's jealous of the way he is honorable, honest and expansive as a person.

"It's almost embarrassing because you know, we're all human, right? And he's human, but to see someone work and perform at that, that, that high super-human level, you just, like, "Okay, wow. The bar has been raised!" And you know, you're just in awe. You're in awe how someone can constantly keep creating these high levels of perfection over and over and over again. Because we all strive for it. I don't know anyone who doesn't. But to see someone do it over and over again, you're like, "Okay, wow! Who is this person?!"
- Tom Cummins, Entrepreneur

Mr. Miscavige actually holds his own and ensures that millions are given help every year. That's why he is looked up to by religious scholars, Scientologists and those who are working with their supported humanitarian efforts.

"David Miscavige fought so many battles to protect our right to a religion, which is everyone's right."
- Kannon Feshbach, VP Administration Research Firm

Leah definitely looked up to Mr. Miscavige while she was active in Scientology. I have no doubts on this statement; I have listened to her interviews.

She took the wrong route when she wanted to know more about him. How? She could've asked the Church officials at the Scientology Celebrity Centre in Los Angeles. This Church provides an environment that's safe and distraction free to those who are

Scientologists that are in the Arts.

> **"Mr. Miscavige was the most caring and considerate and awesome individual that you could work for."**
> - Valerie Haney, Assistant for Leah Remini

The apostates want to diminish Miscavige's reputation as they want this status for themselves. This is something they are never going to achieve. This fact haunts them every day.

> **"I know David Miscavige personally. As such I know him to be completely honest, and sincerely dedicated to helping people."**
> - Mike Rinder (stated under penalty of perjury)

Mr. Miscavige has accomplished milestones that have never been attempted by any other religion. His accomplishments have been recognized by religious scholars, government officials and humanitarians.

> **"David Miscavige gives Scientology, like, the image, like, the standard, OK? When you look at him and you see how he behaves in life, how he treats people, how he operates —no matter what area of life, whether it's his personal life or his professional life—in any given situation, he epitomizes what L. Ron Hubbard put in place as "This would be a Scientologist, this would be the actions that a Scientologist would take, how a Scientologist would behave." - Diane Stein, Human Rights Advocate**

> **"The sheer volume of despicable allegations made about him (David Miscavige) are intended to create the false impression that where there is smoke there is fire."**
> - Mike Rinder (stated under penalty of perjury)

Does Scientology's Leader care about his staff? Are the allegations that attackers make actually valid?

> **"A number of years ago, I think about ten, it's about**

ten years ago now that my sister, my younger sister sadly passed away, and her name was Susie and we were, we'd been very close as brother and sister and it was quite a big hole in my life at the time.

And there was a memorial service at Saint Hill and I was astonished to see that there was this enormous bouquet of flowers that the Chairman of the Board, Mr. Miscavige, had sent over for Susie, which was very touching. And then I was handed a letter from him asking me if I was okay and if I needed anything to get in contact with him and I was very touched by the compassion and considering how many people he must meet in his life.

To have taken that much trouble, it meant a huge amount and it shows a side to him that not only do we have the benefit of his leadership and his direction and all of the things that that had bought us."
- Gray Levett, Founder, Grays of Westminster

"On many occasions I have seen David go out of his way to help others. I well recall two times where I took ill and it was David who called the doctor and personally ensured that everything possible was done to help me recover."
- Mike Rinder (stated under penalty of perjury)

While I know there are many others that have stated good things about Mr. Miscavige, I believe statements that are made under penalty of perjury should be seen as more than just testimonials.

"Question: So, the only person you told lies to during the time you were at the Church of Scientology was Mr. Miscavige, correct?

"Mike Rinder: Yeah, that's correct."

(Stated during a deposition, under penalty of perjury in the United States of America)

The statements made under penalty of perjury in the United States of America were not made under duress, altered and they weren't made with any lack of knowledge.

Mike Rinder had the information at his fingertips. He was working with Mr. Miscavige. Mike was holding the position of the International Scientology Spokesperson. This is a position that works with Mr. Miscavige on a daily basis.

The statements made recently under oath contradict the statements made here and should be considered at once as committing perjury. You cannot claim the statements made after expulsion are true, especially when you are paid to lie about the Church.

How would Mike know what is going on in Scientology right now? How would Leah know? The best information they have is from the 1990's and that's about 30 years ago.

Leah's obsession isn't just about David Miscavige but has escalated into an assault on his wife as well. Leah and Mike are following each other along the path of attacking the Church for money. Read on for more.

CHAPTER 8: WHERE IS SHELLY?

Remini and her attackers are using "Where's Shelly" as a go to public relations statement. It was started before Leah became an attacker of Scientology. Tony Ortega and Mike Rinder have been pushing this statement forever.

Shelly Miscavige is not missing. This is shocking for those who are tricked into believing this.

This is actually a statement that Leah kept pushing with hope that Mr. Miscavige or an official from Scientology would say something about it and go against what the Leader's wife agreed to. This would expose herself and open herself for attacks by the public and the media.

This is a publicity stunt led by Leah. Mike Rinder and Tony Ortega are just following her lead.

This statement is easily discredited by Leah herself. Here's a conversation with Mark Rathbun, Mike Rinder, and Leah Remini:

> **"One of the critical parts of the Rinder, Ortega, Remini roll-out of Remini was the "missing" Shelly Miscavige, the wife of David Miscavige. And you know, at the time, in 2013, I think it was, Rinder told me about that, that she was going to**

do a whole thing about "where's Shelly" and put the Church in just an unbelievable terrible position because, you know, he figured it all out because he'd been in public relations his entire life. And he figured it all out there was going to be this untenable position where nobody could respond to it because it is so personal and it's so—the accusation is so, one of those things—like a "do you [still] beat your wife" conundrum, right? The way they're framing the accusation that they could just go to town and make it into a series—a serial—that just keeps playing out. Right?

And I said, "Mike, why would Leah do something like this, you know, if she has any concern about her own credibility and integrity? You know she's not missing. You know that Leah Remini truly doesn't have the rank to ask to know exactly where she is, when, and how she does her business. That just as much as she feels like, you know, that she needs the ability to be wherever she wants and associate with whomever she wants, Shelly has the exact same right. And you know that the last person in the world she'd want to see is Leah Remini or Mike Rinder."

Mike goes, "Yeah, yeah, I know, I know, I know all that but it's like this perfect thing because it puts them in a position where this is the wife of the head of Scientology. It puts them in this untenable position."

He knew. He knew it was a scam from the beginning. He knew it was a cheap shot from the beginning.

I was certain that Rinder conned her on the Shelly story being a story of manufacture and then when I called her out on it, she said, "Oh yeah, I already knew that. I was running a false black PR campaign the entire time."

I said, "You know, Mike Rinder knows this is a scam and a sham. And if you had asked me about it and asked my opinion you wouldn't have gotten into this in the first place."

> She goes, "I know that, I knew she wasn't missing."
> In other words, she told me she is in complete and
> utter league and agreement with Mike Rinder.
>
> At that time I was just giving her the benefit of the
> doubt, maybe she was just being taken advantage of
> because Mike—you know, that's what he is famous for
> —he's the most agreeable guy on the planet and people
> find that reassuring to have him around them, so he is
> making good, regular bucks by playing that role for her.
> But no, she knew that. That was cool with her. In other
> words, she knew it was a scam from the beginning.
>
> The amazing thing is—that was 2014, '15, '16—we're
> three years later and they're still running it. Every several
> months or so they roll the thing out again, they come out
> with an event—a PR event. She'll file an FOI request with
> the police. And Ortega will run this big thing and try to get
> it out to the tabloids. She's complaining because the police
> aren't investigating the Shelly thing, right. They get their
> documents, their responses, no further story, right? Because
> there's nothing there. But they don't inform the troll farm
> —all these people living in this alternate reality—that they
> believe this world view that they are being fed by Remini,
> Rinder and Ortega who are laughing all the way to the bank."

You can see that Leah basically made this up with Mike Rinder and Tony Ortega. It's false and it's done for publicity and it's a waste to law enforcement's time and resources.

No matter whom you are who you think you are and what you've done, you've got to understand that respecting law enforcement is a priority.

People who follow this story as reality need to wake up and smell the cow dung. It is unrealistic and it's there to make money and popularity.

Shelly Miscavige is not missing and here is a statement from the LAPD:

"The investigation has been closed and we consider the report to be unfounded."

Why? Three hours after the report was filed in 2013 (a month after the Church expelled Leah) they found her at her residence, alive and well. The LAPD wasted 3+ hours following a case that was falsely reported. This time could've been spent stopping a crime from happening, protecting a LA school from shooters, and even stopping a speeding car or a reckless driver. You get the idea.

These are the kind of reports that shouldn't be allowed to persist and be publicized as an "actual matter". Leah, Mike and Tony have no idea how important law enforcement's time is and they will continue as long as they keep getting paid for this negative attention.

This needs to stop, it has happened since 2013 when her obsession with Mr. Miscavige grew even larger as Scientology expelled her. Today she has no way of contacting him or Scientology.

Here is a piece from Scientology's documentation on Leah Remini and the Shelly Miscavige con:

"After her tabloid-orchestrated departure announcement, Remini's first move was to file a false "missing persons" report in August 2013 to harass the wife of the leader of the religion. It was part of a harassment campaign cooked up with bullies Mike Rinder, Marc and Claire Headley and Tony Ortega. Remini used an acquaintance of hers in the LAPD to personally file the report, which she quickly leaked to the media. But it all blew up in her face when the LAPD took the extraordinary step of thoroughly debunking to the media Remini's absurd claim within hours, calling it "unfounded." Remini wasted valuable

public resources in an attempt to viciously harass the Church leader's wife, whom Ms. Remini has obsessively stalked.

Within hours, what had been a gloating Remini turned red-faced with embarrassment when the LAPD closed the case. Unable to admit or accept she was wrong, Remini continues unsuccessfully to try to spread her myth. There is no goodwill in her actions. Her false reports have nothing to do with a big heart. They have to do with the burning resentment usually only found in a cast aside, vindictive and bitter ex-wife."

CHAPTER 9: THE ULTIMATE FAILURE OF LEAH REMINI

A fter finding out that Scientology really hasn't done any illegal activities, Remini needed to invent some and who better than to work with on this than Mike Rinder. Mike lied to the Leader of Scientology more times than he could count.

"**On March 9, 1997, I met attorney Ken Dandar for the first time when I participated in a picket in Clearwater, Florida, against the Church of Scientology. Mr. Dandar had an extensive discussion ... at that meeting in my presence to learn about the pursuit of other Scientology corporations and church leaders as a litigation tactic to 'go after' Scientology.**"
- Robert Minton

Leah and her posse actually went through the past records of all of the lawsuits that people who are either Anti-Scientology or were convinced that Scientology was the fault for their situation. This encouraged them to find people filing "wrongful death suits" on the religion.

"**It was my observation and intent that the LMT (Lisa**

McPherson Trust) was not only the vehicle designated to receive the proceeds of the wrongful death case, it was also used to avoid discovery in the case and disguise the fact that witnesses were being paid. The LMT, represented by Mr. Dandar, maintained that it was separate from the wrongful death case in order to avoid discovery and prevent witnesses from being deposed. Mr. Dandar filed many motions on behalf of LMT and me to try to prevent discovery requests from going forward. The truth was that LMT was inextricably linked to this litigation."
- Robert Minton

Therefore, here is what they ended up doing to the poor families of these innocent people who had a medical condition and for whatever reason were not attending to it. They blasted their family members and church officials that were not around at the time of these horrific incidents and would never have let this happen.

"I contacted Mr. Dandar in October 1997 and offered to loan the Estate $100,000 to defray costs and expenses so this case could become a vehicle to attack Scientology on a broad scale.

"That $100,000 and all subsequent amounts, up to a total of $2,050,000 I loaned to the Estate, was specifically for covering the expenses of litigating the wrongful death case."
- Robert Minton

Yes, these are tragic incidents and cannot be brushed aside, but they really don't need to be brought back up for publicity reasons. Using someone's death as a pawn to attack the religion is *very low*. It is actually lower than calling the religion a cult. And, that's low.

"Mr. Dandar also told me he did not want the money to appear to come from me because my financial involvement was making the case too messy and that he wanted to conceal the money from his employees, Dr. Garko and Tom Haverty, to justify cutting back payments to them. He told me I should never disclose these funds were from me. From this point forward, Mr. Dandar told me that he would tell his employees he was funding the litigation from his retirement account.

"Following these conversations with Mr. Dandar about the $500,000, I caused a check dated May 1, 2000, in that amount to be issued to Mr. Dandar by the Union Bank of Switzerland, payable at Chase Manhattan Bank in New York. I handed this check to Mr. Dandar at the Bombay Bicycle Club in Clearwater, Florida, a few days after May 1, 2000."
- Robert Minton

But, here is what occurred with these suits. The truth is that the persons involved were never actually told by the church or any of its officials to not seek medical attention nor were they told how to live their lives. These persons were not told to do anything that would remotely harm them, they are instructed to let the member or the visitor be and to deliver any course or service that they desire and that's it.

"But then what started happening was after he stopped funding the case, a lot of the critics who were working with Mr. Dandar just totally turned on Mr. Minton and me and really put us in a situation where it was a worse attack against us than even what was happening from Scientology or what they had ever done." and "[T]he anti-Scientologists have been angrier at us and more threatening at us and more intimidating of us than Scientology ever even thought of being. I'm not kidding."
- Robert Minton

Therefore, these suits were already handled with the Courts and were already handled with the respective parties because, although it was tragic and that it happened at or near the Church, it was not the church's fault and that is what it boils down to.

These stories only create controversy and that is exactly what

Leah and her posse want. These deaths are tragic but, pawning it off on some conspiracy against the religion is really low and frankly needs to be stopped. Nobody needs money and publicity *that bad.*

> **"Several weeks before my deposition on May 24, 2000, I had several conversations with Mr. Dandar regarding additional funds he said he needed for the trial of the wrongful death case. He asked me for enough money to take him through the trial. He told me an additional $500,000 would be sufficient. He told me he had a way to hide the funds from Scientology and told me I should arrange payments in such a way that the funds could not be traced back to me. He told me he would not put these funds in his client trust account and that he had another account that Scientology could never find."**
> - Robert Minton

In fact, I am sure people would pay dearly to keep these sad stories off the TV screen and out of the tabloids. It only acts to smear the person's name all over the place and it is smearing the family's tragic moment around and having them re-experience the devastating loss of their loved one due to whatever personal decision or circumstance he/she made. There are unfortunate events everywhere, in fact someone can sensationalize people who pass away at Amusement Parks and even in Disneyland.

> **"I gathered the most vocal Scientology critics and most of the anti-Scientology witnesses under the umbrella of the LMT [Lisa McPherson Trust]. I paid the witnesses through my funding of the LMT and put other critics on the LMT Board of Advisors. Because I was funding both the case and its witnesses, the wrongful death case and the LMT became virtually interchangeable."**
> - Robert Minton

One mother stood up to Leah and her posse after throwing their daughter's name and her devastating decision and circumstance on the TV screen for attention and publicity. In fact, she was so upset that she was actually crying and her son also had a few words to say.

These people are actually brave to want to stand up for their daughter against a bunch of emotionless and careless monsters that choose money and fame over honesty and care. In this example I personally know these family members as well as their daughter.

The gal that passed on was not upset with Scientology and was not upset with L. Ron Hubbard. She loved Scientology and actually convinced me to keep on moving in Scientology because she believed that it was the best thing anybody could do in the world.

She had disagreements with certain friends of her and she was not able to come to an agreement with these individuals. But, these individuals had actually discovered that she had reverted to drugs and she dated one of them who was very concerned. I was able to mend some of the disagreement between them but, she used this as a reason to do more drugs.

After a time it was no longer about the disagreement or upset anymore, it was about motivating herself to take more drugs. She was addicted and she did not want help to get off of them. Her mother and brother invested every dime into different programs, both Scientology and non-Scientology related. Nothing was helping because she wasn't accepting of it. Her mother was her best friend and she was there for her up to the end. She had been living in Los Angeles at that time.

I will always miss having quesadillas and lemonade with her, but I know that she is no longer suffering the pain of addiction and I know that she is in a happier place. I am very sorry that it ended that way and I really wish that she was around still but some things you can't change because you don't want to force the person to do anything the person doesn't want to do.

This is what the brother has to say about it all:

"This whole show, you know, bringing my sister into this and dragging all this through the mud is really – it's appalling.

"I mean I can't believe that somebody would do that."

This is what the mother has to say about it:

"I find it incredibly offensive and incredibly hurtful that I've had to go through this absolute hell that happened to me and my family.

"And, now this woman, Leah Remini, and this very selfish man, Tony Ortega, want to prey on someone who's had to go through this tragedy and bring it back again.

"For me to have to relive, go through and be criticized for which is a really, really low blow. That they could actually go after people that have had to go through something like this, just tells you who Leah Remini and Tony Ortega really are."

What does this have to do with Remini? Why do I mention this? They're using the deaths of Scientologists a pawn against Scientology. Scientologists are human beings and they deserve respect. That is all that needs to be stated.

Scientology doesn't cure diseases, illnesses, or physical ailments in any way. It is an applied religious philosophy founded on the work of 50,000 years of working men and women.

Scientologists are not supposed to be the perfect example of health, they are just like you and I, we all want the best health. Sometimes you can't plan diseases.

The statements that they use against Scientology regarding these cases are sick. These individuals are evil and sick minded. Nobody should have to experience what these individuals have experienced even after their deaths.

There was no wrongdoing on behalf of the Church of Scientology. The Church doesn't control <u>any</u> Scientologist's personal decisions medically or in general.

Scientologists are against Psychiatry for their abuses in the field of mental health and will not tolerate the abuses of their friends, family, and strangers. So, Scientologists seek alternative treatment either by Scientology Counseling or simply meeting with a Physician or Medical Doctor.

There is no rule in Scientology that states how you live your life. There are moral codes and those are to be followed if you'd like to live a happy and successful life. If you don't, you don't need to bother with it.

Leah Remini, Mike Rinder, and Tony Ortega are the ones pushing the false narratives of their small cult members and loyal followers. They don't need to believe it; they just need to push it out there to get their paycheck from their masters.

CHAPTER 10: THE PERFECT SCIENTOLOGY FAMILY

The family aspect of Leah's life is not ideal. It is far from that, and believe it or not her family started off happily as a Scientology family. Now her family is distant, disconnected (based on her doing) and unsuccessful. This dynamic in Leah's life is nonexistent. It is confused and destroyed; it is hard to state that she has a family dynamic at all.

Her father George was ill and he needed $1,500 for an operation that would help treat the illness, with hopes of getting better. Leah committed to helping him pay for it, and then completely backed out. This caused her father to panic to find a way to afford it after all he had done for her.

After this, their relationship started to deteriorate faster than before. George had Leah's back and she didn't have his at the time when he needed it. Based on his care level, he would have done everything in his power to help her if she needed it.

After being expelled from Scientology, Leah left with her

mother. George and his now ex-wife split up as one wanted to continue being a Scientologist and the other did not. The mother didn't even want George to have an interest in it anymore and that is not what he wanted.

Leah's step-sister at the time was going through some major decisions and basically led up to her death at an early age of mid-twenties. Leah wasn't there.

The step-mother called Leah and spoke about it. By the end of the call, Leah had paid for the funeral.

As you can see, this is contrary to what Scientology promotes regarding the Family Dynamic. Scientologists are happy with their families and are always in support of their families and expansion and improvement. When upsets arise there are basic, simple tools that people can use to help repair the situation.

In my family, we are Scientologists. We are held to the belief and mindsets that we are to make sure each of us are doing well and are improving in life. If we aren't, we see to it that the relative gets the help he/she requires and continues to improve and win in life. The family unit is one of the main parts of Scientology and it is one of their core beliefs and practices.

As Mr. Hubbard states about Family,

"The Second Dynamic is CREATIVITY.

Creativity is making things for the future and the Second Dynamic includes any creativity. The Second Dynamic contains the family unit and raising children as well as anything that can be categorized as a family activity. It also, incidentally, includes sex as a mechanism to compel future survival."

Therefore, this quote establishes the Second Dynamic in the Eight Dynamics of Scientology. Here are the others, for reference.

The First Dynamic is SELF.

This is the effort to survive as an individual, to be an individual. It includes one's own body and one's own mind. It is the effort to attain the highest level of survival for the longest possible time for self. This dynamic includes the individual plus his immediate possessions. It does not include other people. It is the urge to survive as one's self. Here we have individuality expressed fully.

The Second Dynamic is CREATIVITY.

Creativity is making things for the future and the Second Dynamic includes any creativity. The Second Dynamic contains the family unit and raising children as well as anything that can be categorized as a family activity. It also, incidentally, includes sex as a mechanism to compel future survival.

The Third Dynamic is GROUP SURVIVAL.

This is the urge to survive through a group of individuals or as a group. It is group survival with the group tending to take on a life and existence of its own. A group can be a community, friends, a company, a social lodge, a state, a nation, a race or any group. It doesn't matter what size this group is, it is seeking to survive as a group.

The Fourth Dynamic is SPECIES.

Man's Fourth Dynamic is the species of Mankind. This is the urge toward survival through all Mankind and as all Mankind. Whereas the American nationality would be considered a Third Dynamic for Americans, all the nationalities of the world together would be considered the Fourth Dynamic. All men and women, because they are men and women, seek to survive as men and women and for men and women.

The Fifth Dynamic is LIFE FORMS.

This is the urge to survive as life forms and with the help of life forms such as animals, birds, insects, fish and vegetation. This includes all living things whether animal or vegetable, anything directly and intimately motivated by life. It is the effort to survive for any and every form of life. It is the interest in life as such.

The Sixth Dynamic is the PHYSICAL UNIVERSE.

The physical universe has four components. These are matter, energy, space and time. The Sixth Dynamic is the urge of the physical universe to survive, by the physical universe itself and with the help of the physical universe and each one of its component parts.

The Seventh Dynamic is the SPIRITUAL DYNAMIC.

This is the urge to survive as spiritual beings or the urge for life itself to survive. Anything spiritual, with or without identity, would come under the heading of the Seventh Dynamic. It includes one's beingness, the ability to create, the ability to cause survival or to survive, the ability to destroy or pretend to be destroyed. A subheading of this dynamic is ideas and concepts and the desire to survive through these. The Seventh Dynamic is life source. This is separate from the physical universe and is the source of life itself. Thus, there is an effort for the survival of life source.

The Eighth Dynamic is the urge toward existence as INFINITY.

The Eighth Dynamic also is commonly called God, the Supreme Being or Creator, but it is correctly defined as infinity. It actually embraces the allness of all. That is why, according to L. Ron Hubbard, "when the Seventh Dynamic is reached in its entirety, one will only then discover the true Eighth Dynamic."

This is all available in the books of Scientology written by L. Ron Hubbard, Scientology: The Fundamentals of Thought. This is a great book that goes over the life aspects in Scientology and Dianetics for beginners.

For moral and ethical conduct, Scientologists are attracted to

Introduction to Scientology Ethics and The Way to Happiness. Anything about these topics and codes that have to do with conduct, beliefs and practices are found in these books mentioned.

CHAPTER 11: EMOTIONAL AFTERMATH

S ome of Leah's relatives have actually spoken out against her, about what she is doing and what she has done in her life. They do this because they are outraged by her blatant lies and attacks on the Church. These people are brave in their own right and I am giving them a platform and a voice without hesitation or reservation.

I know I am not liked or admired by others for spreading this side of someone but it needs attention with any public figure. Every public figure has an image and that image is correctly established with truth and not lies. These are not made up or fake news.

So these are some of their stories…

"Leah once told me—I had to be tested for cancer—and Leah said, "How much is it?" I said, "It's $1,500."

$1,500 is a pair of shoes for her. Or boots, that's for $1,500.

And being that my ex-wife was robbing every penny from the company, we were like bad off.

So I turned around and I said, "Leah could you do this for me? You know, it is serious, biopsy for cancer."

She says: "Yeah, yeah, I'll take care of it. What's the doctor's number, what's his name?"

I gave her everything. She said "I'm going to just put it on my credit card." I says, "fine."

Leah never did it. I say, "Why didn't you do it?" "Well I don't want them to have my credit card number." I said, "Why don't you send him a money order, overnight?" She says, "I didn't think of that."

I say, "You are talking about my life here for $1,500." So she says, "What can I do," blablablabla. I said "alright, drop it, forget it."

- George Remini, Father of Leah Remini

This is a serious matter about Leah's father dealing with cancer. He is talking about the lack of support he received from Leah, his daughter. It is very important to any father that his family has his back as well.

Leah Remini is not thinking about others, which includes her own family. I mean her father would've done anything and everything for her. If she were sick and on the verge of needing to be tested for cancer, he would've found a way to make sure that she got that treatment, even if it would have cost his remaining years working to pay it off. He would have done it.

Leah is the one disconnecting families and she started with her own.

Donna Fiore, former step-mother of Leah Remini, spoke to the National Enquirer in January 2014. Leah ended up snubbing her dying step-sister. How could she do this?

"Leah turned her back on Stephanie while she

was dying, and I am furious about it!"…

"Ignored Stephanie's pleas for help"

Stephanie died on New Year's Eve. She died. This is sickening that she would do such a thing. This is incredibly morbid.

- - -

Here is what her father has stated in regards to her carelessness and her lies.

"You are still the same person you were in Brooklyn. Except you have money and a home, you're still a self-centered bitch. Everyone around you knows that but because their survival depends on you they really don't say what's really on their mind."

- - -

This is what Leah's stepfather stated in July of 2012 in regards to her problems with family members:

"Leah's sister (younger) Shannon was in tears 3 weeks ago … she was talking about how hard it was working for Leah lately. How critical she was about her work in the house office … In the last 3 months she has fired her mother at least twice. Vicki has quit her post 2 or 3 times because of her critical argument over house things… Shannon has been fired a few times."
- George Marshall

In the same report, George also stated this regarding her marriage with her husband, Angelo Pagan:

"Angelo has said a few times [in] the past 4 months she doesn't want to be married anymore to him."

These are Leah's relatives and they despise of the way she handled problems, her carelessness towards her family, and the inability to take responsibility (unless persuaded to).

That is the truth about Leah. This is not her publicity front. This is who she is.

CHAPTER 12:
SPIES LIKE US

N ow, Leah may act nice, friendly, and otherwise just care about people for what they state. But, you'd be incorrect to follow this train of thought without having this information.

I do not normally share personal details but, when I came across this in researching Leah Remini and her history – I couldn't pass it up as people need to spread some awareness on this topic... This action is frowned upon in an ethical society and with sane people who truly believe marriage and family are the foundation to a bettered society and a happy community.

In 1997, Leah Remini had an affair with Angelo Pagan, who was already married to Raquel Pagan who has a son, Alex Pagan.

In an interview with Star Magazine, Raquel states about Leah Remini's affair with Angelo, "cold heartedly wooed her husband" and "didn't care about destroying a family. "This was while the situation was still going on and the entire situation was trying to mend itself or come out with a decision.

"Leah didn't care about destroying a family."
—Raquel Pagan

Above are the statements from Raquel Pagan from the divorce court.

Interestingly enough, Leah and Angelo were eventually married in 2003. But, what led up to this result was not easy and was attacks after attacks from Leah to Raquel. Eventually making her apathetic and cower down to the fact that Angelo was already over her because of the following actions she took.

This is an actual statement by Leah Remini in 1999 regarding her hiring a private investigator so that he finds something on

Raquel that she can use against her in her conversations with Angelo. This would be used in the upcoming conversations so that she could convince him that she was better than Raquel and to make sure that the final decision was that of divorce from Raquel.

When she was digging up dirt on Raquel, Raquel was trying to find out what was going on from her son and his friends at school. Raquel declared in divorce court that she had found out that Alex Pagan (Raquel and Angelo's son) had been in trouble at school for talking about **"naked girls and sex"** but when she found out more about it she found out that he and his friends knew that after a certain hour **"porn comes on the TV at Dad's house"**. This, being his mother, made her a bit upset and she had to share it.

(Star Magazine article covering Raquel's tell-all about
Leah Remini and her affair with Angelo.)

Leah's explanation for all of this was actually quite sinister and
very terribly executed. This was actually one of the attempts
that she had made to try to tear up the relationship between Angelo and Raquel and that were a success. Sadly, Angelo chose to
stick with Leah after all the "dirt digging".

Next, Leah's attempt at ensuring that neither Raquel nor Angelo's mother could see Angelo and Alex. This shocking declaration about the secret attack from Leah after a private call with
Angelo turns ugly.

> **"...it was used by Angelo and Ms. Remini as a revenge, for
> taking Angelo to court... They began to prevent me from any
> contact with my son. Ms. Remini even interrupted a private
> conversation I had with my son Alex by phone. She began to
> shout out profanity and insults against not only me but also
> against Angelo's ex-wife, Raquel. She went as far as to tell me
> that she was going to make sure that I did not speak with my
> son Alex and that she would make sure I would not see him
> again."**
> - Mother of Angelo Pagan

This was not only the last leg of the divorce situation but, it was
the attempt that was not successful in the courtroom. Angelo
and Leah didn't win this match and with Leah's evil tendencies
it was officially declared unsuccessful.

She makes baseless threats and doesn't follow through with

them. Just like her statements on truth and exposing, she never really tends to know neither what she is talking about nor what she is doing.

Therefore, this information is necessary to form an understanding of who Remini is truly and why she is hiding this side from the public.

If she is so "honest" and "brave", why isn't she brave enough to come clean on the past and make it known among the rest of her experiences and intentional destruction attempts. There is a side to her that not many people know about; this is what I am addressing on top of everything else that these one-minded apostates do.

Angelo, its okay to contact us for help...just saying.

CHAPTER 13: COMPARISON

There are a few pushing this statement:

> **"Ryan is a young Scientologist. He doesn't know any-thing about the religion. He is only doing this be-cause…"**

I can understand the confusion. I can understand the doubt.

I don't represent Scientology. I am only a Scientologist. I prac-tice and use the tools of the religion. I use it because it works.

This doesn't mean that I haven't tried other techniques, prin-ciples and tools. It doesn't mean I have only had experienced Scientology and have been "prevented" from experiencing other faiths and paths. It doesn't mean I don't believe in the other religions I embrace as are traditional to my family.

I have found Scientology to be the stable part of my life. It has helped me in ways that complement Christianity and other basic studies.

I have relatives that are of different faiths. It's very spiritual.

Leah has only pretended to be a Scientologist. She has hated it with a passion since she was 14; this is per the conversations with her former friends.

Leah has only participated in humanitarian programs, donated just a little to Scientology, did some services (if she felt like it), took over people's houses, caused Scientologists to stop helping others, she's racist and more.

"She called my son a "nigglet," which is like, the junior, like, "nigger." I had no idea that she was so evil this way. And the stories that I started to hear that she would say that I lived in a really dirty home and … she was just talking really negatively and horribly about me to others. And everybody started coming to me and telling me these things and I was devastated. And I didn't even know that this was how she really felt about me. I start… I could tell here and there she would say really nasty things like covertly to me and we would get into big fights and we were just… We would fight and make-up, fight and make-up. It was like I was in an abusive relationship.

"(When she departed Scientology) I pleaded with her and she didn't even answer me. She's the one that disconnected from people all the time. She would change her number all the time. Every time. As soon as she got upset with somebody, she wouldn't talk to them anymore. This was her way. This was her modus operandi. So now she's trying to flip it to make herself be the victim.

"For her to go around and say, "Oh! I'm so devastated. The god… I'm the godmother of my friend's children and she disconnected from me and she hurt me." That's bull!"
- Stacy, Former Friend

Leah is disconnecting from people, I don't disconnect from friends. I disconnect from those who harm, attack, hate, and commit crimes and other contra-survival actions. Stacy was Leah's good friend. You can tell Stacy cared for her. You can see it from the way she is stating her disagreement.

I do not create upsets with friends and then disconnect. This is irresponsible. This is Leah's trademark move. She will push the blame on someone else.

Leah and Mike are perfect for each other. They have both messed up things for themselves and the Church.

I am not perfect. I have taken responsibility for any misdeeds. This puts me an infinite amount of steps ahead of Leah. This scares those who have committed wrongdoings. If they only knew that life doesn't have to be that dark and lonesome.

This is what a person said about some work I've done:

"I don't know what you did but I feel amazing. I am ready to go back out there for my next shift.

"I haven't been getting good sleep since the fires started. I am gonna sleep real well tonight. I feel like I finally have energy."
- Firefighter, Carr Fire

It takes the same amount of effort to help someone as it does to harm someone. Trust me, I have done it myself.

I was in a very horrid relationship. I could've blamed it solely on her, I didn't. I ended up taking responsibility for my wrong-doings and ending it the right way.

The Church of Scientology doesn't interfere with the relationships of others. The Scientology principles are for use in people's lives for improvement. This is not legal assistance in matters of divorce, break-up and other aspects of relationships.

The word Scientology means the study of truth, the study of life. These are tools to better your life, not to control you or tell you how to lead one's life.

Families especially are *very* important to Scientologists. If there's a rift between someone in a family, the principles are able to be applied to help handle that rift.

I have had conversations with Scientology officials. I have had specific conversations about religious converts. There is no such thing. I was tricked to believe this was something that was occurring by Leah Remini. Scientology is all-denominational and people can be Atheist, Buddhist, Jewish, Muslim, Christian with zero contradictions.

I have been on Staff at the Church of Scientology in Portland, Oregon. I have helped many people through the courses and the literature. I have never once changed someone's religion.

I have respect for religions. I know that people have the right to their religious beliefs and practices. I know that Scientology isn't here to change that.

Specifically, L. Ron Hubbard states:

"Change no man's religion..." - L. Ron Hubbard

I would recommend reading *Scientology: The Fundamentals of Thought* by L. Ron Hubbard. This book was written for those studying Scientology's basic principles.

CHAPTER 14: LEAH
IS COLLECTING

T he information presented here is based on the agenda of the attackers. This is a valid agenda and is based on the interviews of Mark "Marty" Rathbun. This is what she leveraged into her hate show on A&E Networks.

Does one work without an agenda? Does one actually have a purpose in life or a purpose in the route that they are taking in life? Yes, everyone has this in common regardless of religion, gender, opinion, nationality, and race.

Leah has an agenda. This is her unfiltered and complete agenda against her former religion. Why? It stems from her expulsion due to her unprofessional, immoral conduct and her deception in working with fellow Scientologists.

1. Pretend the departure from Scientology was an "escape" and use buzzwords to create chaos and publicity. Otherwise contribute to spreading false propaganda about Scientology.

2. Ride the wave of this publicity as stated in (1) and claim that Scientology is trying to salvage her. This should get investment attention, news attention and gain religious bigots' attention for the greatest campaign in bigot history.

3. Promote that I am speaking out against my former religion as

I can make sure that people start inviting me to meetings, conferences, events, TV interviews, talk shows, radio stations, and even as far as YouTube interviews and videos.

4. Get a corporation to support me so that I can have an opportunity to get famous and generate income as I am out of work and declining.

Also, make sure that this corporation is willing to act against the religion. Ignore all attempts to communicate the truth and facts that will otherwise counter the efforts of the agenda.

5. Write the religion a public demand of $1,500,000 for my silence. The information that I will be using against them is what has been unproven for the last 40 years.

6. Since Scientology declined the offer many times, start pushing those false allegations.

7. Start interviewing with threats. Make it look like I have a lot going on in "exposing" Scientology.

8. Contact those trying to do honest work in society through the media and through the arts. Convince them that Scientology is horrible and needs to be stopped.

9. Contact those who are Anti-Scientology because they were expelled and ride the wave of complete bigotry.

The list is all motivated by **MONEY.**

CHAPTER 15: A&E NETWORKS AND LEAH REMINI

L eah Remini has long since had a way of causing so much disruption, spreading rumors, and blackmailing people to get her way. This is definitely true in the case of A&E Networks and her series on "exposing" her former religion.

The timing was almost perfect when she decided to publicly "leave" Scientology, even though she was expelled and then she posed it as "leaving". She used this expulsion as a publicity stunt and made it seem as if she was a big deal in Scientology and that Scientology was trying to get her to come back so they could fix something they handled wrong with her.

In actuality, Leah Remini was expelled and Scientology doesn't help expelled people. They have already tried to help the person and they haven't been able to get across to the person and so, the person will continue to do the things that are against the codes in Scientology.

The Church made no attempt at "handling" or "salvaging" anything with her. She was gone to them and Scientologists were thrilled that she was gone. She was a pretender and she always worked on lying to others about things that she didn't do or did do whatever the case was at the time.

There were moments when she was at an event or a specific Church gathering that she would either show up intoxicated, belligerent, or otherwise in harassment mode against fellow members. She would cause scenes that wouldn't have any basis and she would always request to have venues, spaces, and even rooms made her way otherwise there would be trouble, whatever that meant. She did this with officials and members anywhere and everywhere.

It was always Leah that would take advantage of Scientologists and their willingness to help. They would assist her in her career, get her new gigs, help her by providing her an investment and even sometimes giving her a place to stay at someone's house when she was starting up.

When she was expelled, she decided that she would first harass the Leader of Scientology, David Miscavige by claiming that his wife was missing. She could never get an answer from him or his fellows at the Religious Technology Center because she was already labeled as "obsessed with the Leader" and anything having to do with Mr. Miscavige is kept on the down low due to the fact the officials have a job of protecting Scientologists and its Staff Members *along with* their Religious Order.

Leah doesn't have the authority to ask where Shelly is, where David Miscavige lives, and other such personal questions. Just like I wouldn't have the authority to ask you where you live, what your social security number is, and where your wife or husband is at the moment.

When the Church exposed that she was not missing and that the Los Angeles Police Department found her alive and well, she got very upset and embarrassed and decided to throw the attention back on the Church. She attempted to demand $1,500,000 from the Church, otherwise she would spread gossip, rumors, and lies through the press, news, media, and on TV. The Church declined the offer multiple times.

Leah Remini signed a contract with A&E Networks to "expose" her former religion and was getting ready to bring in the big bucks with her apostate posse. She was already planning to roll out many different episodes on the allegations that Mike Rinder handled personally as the former Scientology Spokesperson.

> **"THR: Leah, I want to turn to you... How much vetting is done of the people who are going to tell their stories on your show? Is that something... Do you have people who have to sort of make them prove their stories?**
>
> **Leah Remini: What... What do you want me to do? 'Prove it to me?' You know? So there is NO VETTING I go take their word for it.**
>
> **THR: And Legal will let you get away with that?**
>
> **Leah Remini: Well they have to. Because they are 'my people'."**

Leah relied on Mike's "expertise" in this area as he knew exactly what the apostates said against his handling and answers (that were 100% truthful) and what caused the cases to be thrown out of Court. He knew what they had said and who to bring back from the past to try to spark some publicity and some profit from his past work in the Church.

> **"Mike Rinder is the bobble-head doll for Remini."**

These were the attempts that were worked out so well that even A&E was banking a pretty good salary but that didn't last very long.

When the Church caught wind of what was happening, the Church stepped in and began bringing those related to the apostates onto the stage and they began writing letters, doing unscripted interviews, vetting all of the information, ensuring that A&E had all documentation of everything that they had already found out about the apostates, the court cases that they had thrown out of Court, and many other binders of information. In fact, the Church literally sent more information than they had sent any other publication, media outlets, and public figure ever and all of it on the Church's dime.

This caused Leah to begin to roll-out more because she knew that it was about to go down in viewers and ratings due to the fact that the Church was onto her agenda and was exposing, *honestly* (unlike Leah and her posse), what their intentions were, what they had actually done, where the cases went, what the people actually knew, and if they were actually Scientologists and also vetted their stories newly so that it was new information and not information found 30 years ago.

Therefore, Leah's agenda is not new and she is now one of the apostates against Scientology trying to stop it from helping people and stopping others from finding out about themselves and others. This is sad for them because they have screwed up so much that they can't experience this relief.

> **"Neither the objective sociological researcher nor the court of law can readily regard the apostate as a credible or reliable source of evidence. He must always be seen as one whose personal history predisposes him to bias..."**
> - Professor Bryan R. Wilson,
> All Souls College at Oxford and the British Academy

No matter what they have stated about Scientology "personally" it is all geared toward a purpose in their agenda.

> **"(These apostates) Present a distorted view of the new religions to the public, the academy, and the courts by virtue of their ready availability and eagerness to testify against their former religious associations and activities. Such apostates always act out of a scenario that vindicates themselves by shifting responsibility for their actions to the religious group... Such apostates can hardly be regarded as**

reliable informants by responsible journalists, scholars, or jurists."
- Dr. Lonnie Kliever, Longtime Professor of Religious Studies at Southern Methodist University

But, this all ties into many other theories that I have been working on in my studies and that I will release at a later date. You might even see it in my next release. It is a massive project and has in it the findings of over 40 years of attacks the apostates have used for years and some of it is phrased or framed a different way but it means the same thing.

You'll find that if you watch the news, listen to interviews, and see the tabloids, these outlets all rely on the best snippets. This is how they form the information to their agenda.

Soundbites are very important for Leah Remini, Mike Rinder, and Tony Ortega. They are also important for anyone from the tabloids, press and dishonest politicians that benefit from fake news distributors.

Leah's episodes on A&E Network were full of these soundbite interviews and they are fed what to say and they are fed when to cry and they definitely got paid for it. This was all an act to get people to believe and to just watch the program so that she and her posse could get paid and get fake attention due to her "bravery".

How do I know this? Well, here is a brave woman that called the Church of Scientology International and who is NOT a Scientologist to alert the church that there is dishonest interviewing going on.

Here is the call transcript:

CHURCH OF SCIENTOLOGY: Church of Scientology International. May I help you?

WHISTLEBLOWER: I don't know very much about

Scientology, so you are going to have to forgive me. I'm not really familiar with it. I was present for a friend of mine while I was on vacation, who was giving an interview for a program and it involved a celebrity named Leah Remini, and I was asked to come over and kind of be there as a support system. So, while I was in the kitchen and this whole crew of people came, and this celebrity that I used to watch on King of Queens came. And she was doing this interview. And during the interview she kept stopping people and telling them, the people I was visiting, and she kept telling them that it needed to be more dramatic, to make it sound as bad as possible. And I was pretty astounded because these were older, what I considered to be older people. And I kind of thought she was taking advantage of them. And I asked at one point during a break my friend if she was really okay with this, and she said yes, and that they were receiving payment for the interview. And I just kind of felt like because she was telling the husband, "You really need to start crying at a certain point. That would be really good." She kept stopping and telling them to up the ante. And she did this while big thing and so it kind of gave me the creeps and made me feel kind of dirty.

- END OF TRANSCRIPT -

This was one of the last interviews they stuffed into the A&E episodes. Ortega, Rinder and Remini are guilty of sound-biting and scripting. Robert Sharenow, Aaron Saidman and Eli Holzman are the ringleaders.

As backed up by the "former guru" Mark "Marty" Rathbun:

"Then they sit down and say 'I really want to find out what happened' right, and then you see these little snippets, all completely distorted and redefined by Remini by Remini providing the narrative. So what happens here is that you have a bit of that 5-10 minutes and then you have cut-out interviews with the same person. In other words, Mike and her are going

and doing this sort of counseling thing, we're gonna sit on the couch and get comfortable. They know to get the juice they got to go back and go who knows who interrogate the person for how many hours, who knows, or rehearse the person.

I don't know but you'll notice they begin on the couch and then they shift to a separate room. Where the guy is individually lit on a set and saying different things. It's a technique that is used throughout the series, clearly the intrepid Rinder and Remini were unable to elicit from the person by just having them tell their narrative enough juicy material to justify an episode on the unreality show. So, they got to go back, put them in a separate session, and do pickups to do the soundbites they need to create the phony narrative."

A sound bite is a short clip of speech or music extracted from a longer piece of audio, often used to promote or show the full length piece.... The insertion of sound bites into news broadcasts or documentaries is open to manipulation, leading to conflict over journalistic ethics.

The above definition shows us that anyone from anywhere can use a video, recording, and even music to manipulate viewers and listeners to thinking something bad or good about a subject. Even to those that don't have tons of time just a couple of sentences of the soundbite will do and that person will be thinking about it and will only duplicate that one thing and will not try to find out more about it.

Leah, Mike and Tony all rely on this in people and in the film crew of A&E. They all know the reason soundbites keep them all being rewarded, pumped with fame, and still backed by some investors. That is really the sole reason they have support.

My duty is to make sure that people are looking at it for what it is and for what it's not.

CHAPTER 16: LEAH'S TABLOID ADVENTURE: PAUL HAGGIS EDITION

Leah has used Paul Haggis' "credibility" in the criminal universe to gain publicity for her attacks against Scientology.

I'd like to dive into who exactly Paul Haggis is and why he was even in Scientology and what he did to Scientologists. He was never a Scientologist, never stated this to his sister either.

Paul Haggis is one of a kind. He robbed Scientologists of their money, time, life, resources, and connections and of their sanity.

"I'm a selfish prick."
- Paul Haggis

Haggis used Scientologists in the entertainment and business industries to get "investments" into his failed projects. He would later default on these projects and pocket the cash.

His own sister used to work with him on his projects and when she caught him on illegal dealings, he'd hurt her physically and mentally. He's a coward.

"Paul was never a Scientologist. Since the beginning he was never a Scientologist, Paul hung around the outskirts of Scientology. The fringe of Scientology. He used our Church, he's used our humanitarian efforts in order to glorify himself and in order to build his career."
- Kathy Haggis, Sister

It has been verified that Paul wasn't a Scientologist through his actions, Scientologists who invested in him and those who tried to offer him some help. He always used Scientologists and never helped them.

Paul was never one you could count on if you needed someone to watch your children, loan you some money, give you some friendly advice and be your friend. He is someone who cares about himself and nobody else.

"Paul got his first job through Scientologists. Paul came and hung out at our Celebrity Center, where there were writers who were already working.

"A very dear friend of mine gave Paul his first job. I was there, I heard the first conversations at the time of Paul very cleverly wheedling his way into a job, so that he could get onto a prime time show. Once Paul got onto that prime time show he managed to find a clever way to dump that writer and move onto another television series and get a solo credit."
- Kathy Haggis, Sister

Haggis isn't a legitimate source of information about Scientology. Haggis is a good source for conning, criminality, fraud and brainwashing. That is what he is good for.

Haggis should become a Psychiatrist, except then he'd have to listen, well at least he could get on board with the outcome with that being money.

There is another part of Haggis' story that nobody has brought up.

Leah and Mike have been slamming Danny Masterson for his accusations, they haven't been silenced, and Danny has only addressed them privately to vet them and to understand how to correct what may or might not have happened. That is between Danny and the complainant.

What about Haggis?

The accusations made about Haggis have been fought and have been attempted to be silenced by Haggis in court. He has tried to silence those speaking out against him with defamation lawsuits. That is how sickening this guy really is. He doesn't even have the balls to confront what he's done.

When the allegations started, Haggis started resigning from charitable organizations he was using for publicity, contracts that he was part of and even people who he was connected with for utilization of their connections and popularity.

One actually spoke out against him anonymously to dispel his rumor line in regards to stating that they were "sent by Scientology". If this were true, Scientology would have stopped them by now. Plus, why would they send people to make false allegations of rape and sexual harassment?

Haggis is dreaming things up to deflect. He needs to stop silencing victims.

> **"I have no connection to Scientology or its practitioners. For those people—including actress Leah Remini—who have stated publicly that all of Haggis' accusers are part of a Scientology conspiracy, shame on you. Isn't now the time to be listening to your sisters? Such baseless statements attempt to silence all of us and the entire #Me Too movement."**
> - Victim, The Hollywood Reporter

"Survivors of sexual violence need their day in court. And that's what's so important about this case. The lower court said yes, survivors do get their day in court and now the defendant is again trying to assert his (Paul Haggis') control and dominance to silence her.... We are proud to sign on to this amicus alongside so many important organizations fighting for justice."
- Carrie Goldberg, owner, victims' rights law firm, C.A. Goldberg, PLLC

CHAPTER 17: ENEMIES OF THE CHURCH

I know I wrote some information regarding the Anti-Scientology Cult in *The Truth about Apostates: The Scientology Story*. I want to provide you with more information, including Remini's role.

The Anti-Scientology Cult (ASC) is a creepy-crawly group of people. These people are connected by their hatred for the Church of Scientology, their lack of a job and their reprehensible history.

Those who are part of their cult cannot talk about anything else but what is on the agenda for the day, week or what's laid out in the future. If they wander from it, they are reprimanded.

> **"They have a website called the 'Outerbanks'. Where the talking points for the day, the week and the future are presented by, particularly by, Rinder and Ortega and their financier, Karen Carriere."**
> - Mark Rathbun

One of their members is Karen and she is a professional prostitute. She has been since the time she was in Scientology. It was one of the factors that got her expelled from Scientology. She was promiscuous and wasn't focused on helping people with

Scientology principles.

Karen is in charge of the money for their cult full of people who are Anti-Scientology. Karen works out deals with disgruntled former members, investors, con-men, criminals and the elderly for their income. The money is then distributed in the accounts of those of the "royalty" and those who have done their share of harassment.

> **She's (Karen Carriere) is the moderator because she is paying the big bucks."**
> - Mark Rathbun

I am sure Karen knows how to control money as she is very knowledgeable about how to roll it in on the streets. She is also very knowledgeable due to having to write checks for failed court cases against Scientology.

> **"You come by invitation only. Only the cream of the crop or as De La Carriere said 'the royalty' gets to be in court."**
> - Mark Rathbun

It is strange how Leah, Mike and Tony state that Scientology isn't a religion. They actually call it a cult. It's hypocritical because by definition THEY are in a cult. Cults are CLOSED groups, and I'm sure they don't allow just you and me to walk in and be part of their activities. Scientology is a wide OPEN group that anyone can join and see the good works for themselves. Hmm, doesn't add up does it.

If only those innocent night show hosts knew what they were involved in. Leah's defamatory statements regarding Scientology were actually about her all along.

I didn't want to expect the worst. I wanted to give Leah a chance. This is just downright distasteful.

> **"This whole Remini production is a complete projection factory. They are a cult, they act like cult members, and they**

project it on Scientology."
- Mark Rathbun

I'm tired of hearing that my religion is a cult. I know this accusation isn't genuine. I know where it comes from. These are some slimy people, no wonder they're part of this cult.

I read that Mark "Marty" Rathbun was part of the "Outer-bankers". I discovered that he was a major contributor to this cult's website. I discovered that Mark had been very neutral.

"Several months later (after declining the offer of being a Producer for the A&E TV show) Leah contacts me and wants me to literally make a commitment to being in the ASC.

"I'm like, I am not a joiner, I am not a sheep, I am not a follower.

"She said 'No no no, it's like if you're against them we're together.

"I said 'You know the problem is you want me to join a group of people that I have had experience with and been involved with that are demonstrably obviously far more unethical, far more disloyal, far more criminal than any Scientologist that I have ever dealt with in 27 years I was in it. And yet, as much as you rail about it you then want me to act in the very way you accuse Scientology of acting.

In other words, if you're not with us, you're with them. I told her no.

Her response was: Not only are you not to get in communication with me again, you must destroy all of my contact information. Because I'm destroying yours."

- Mark Rathbun

The assertion that Scientology is disconnecting people is dishonest. Scientologists choose to disconnect with those he or she wishes to, just like if you have someone in your life who is really bad news and refuses to shape up. You might say 'That's It' and drop them from your social circles and delete them from your phone. That's the simplicity of a 'Disconnection'.

Remini on the other hand disconnects with people who she doesn't agree with. She disconnects from people who won't do what she asks.

Mark recently spoke out against Outerbankers and the Anti-Scientology Cult. He spoke out via YouTube in coordination with the Church of Scientology International. These videos were produced uncoerced and comprise hours of information documenting everything about Leah Remini, Mike Rinder, Tony Ortega, their posse, cult and their agendas.

When Mark released these videos in 2017 and 2018, the Outerbankers and the Anti-Scientology Cult were trying to save their asses. They were trying their best at discrediting. They surrendered.

> **"I got to read you something that was on there (Outerbanks), in fact, I think this was a response to their response to my videos. Somebody pointed out that there were a lot of verifiable facts to my videos (that were critical of Mike Rinder and Tony Ortega).**
>
> **"ATTENTION OUTERBANKERS WE HAVE LONG SINCE HAD RULES AND GUIDELINES... in the rules, we do not permit trashing, or demeaning, or disparaging posts of our hero activist leaders, Mike Rinder and Tony Ortega.**
>
> **"If you attack the main activists, your posts will be deleted. (Censorship) You'll be warned. (Intimidation) If you do not agree to this then you do not belong on Outerbanks. (Disconnection and Expulsion)"**
> - Mark Rathbun

Right after Mark spoke out against the Outerbankers and the ASC, he went through many surprising events. These events were blackmail, harassment, attempts at infiltration and smear campaigns.

> **"Tony Ortega starts a smear campaign and he runs it for six months, nonstop, on me and my family.**

> **"They attempted to infiltrate my family. They attempted to drive wedges between my wife and I, when that failed they literally took up a collection to hire private I's to spy and harass us. And when that failed, they attempted to blackmail me.**

> **"I literally received a blackmail threat. It said if you keep talking about the ASC, if you keep talking about the other side of the story or about our laundry, we are going to expose all of the crimes that you failed to disclose about your experience when you were in Scientology."**
> - Mark Rathbun

If you don't see it by now, I am sure you'll see it eventually. They are projecting everything that they're doing onto Scientology and Scientologists. This is their job.

They are conning people all around the world. They are extorting money from innocent families and hardworking individuals to 'take down' the evil religion. Talk about wasted donations, the return on hate funding is pretty small, plus karma's just waiting at the door to settle things up down the road.

Mark Rathbun didn't end up joining ASC. He is living his life doing whatever he is doing. I hope he is living a more honest life instead of having to live a life of lies, defamation and hate.

Mark ends up exposing a key part in the ASC's agenda. This is so key that they are attacking Mark for even stating this. He probably has to defend himself in court.

> **"The day before Leah Remini's January 2017 20/20 special, what happened was I hear from ABC 20/20 asking me 'Hey, do you know a guy named Sergio?' I**

said 'No, I have never heard of the guy in my life.'

Simultaneously I get an email from Tony Ortega saying 'Sergio Palami says that he got raped by an adult male while he was a teenager in Scientology and that you found out about it and covered it up.'

"I got what was going down, this was the payback on the blackmail. They literally made it up. So, I looked up this Sergio guy, he'd been going on for three or four months in the ASC troll farm.

"So, after I received this email from Tony Ortega, I wrote to ABC 20/20 and stated 'I had never heard of him in my life'.

I understood what was going on, he's running the same op that he's running all the time and Mike Rinder explained it to me 'Tony will run anything because he's got nothing to lose. Because he's a nobody with a blog. Scientology and nobody else is going to waste their time suing a guy who can never make good on whatever damage he does in the first place. And, he can blog from a shopping cart in an alley as well as whatever apartment he's living in now.

So, he's literally got immunity from that respect to libel. What he'll do is, he'll put out the sleaziest criminal innuendo with different grains of truth mixed in and keep repeating it enough with the intention the tabloids at some point will start to pick it up. And, with the intention that he'll keep feeding the tabloid, with the intention that ultimately, in this degraded age of infotainment and click-bait news, the "legitimate media" will pick it up.

"The only reason the blackmail didn't run is because I called ABC out on it. That's how far they went. They blackmailed me, I told them bring it, they had nothing to bring, so they literally manufactured something."
- Mark Rathbun

The Church of Scientology isn't blackmailing anyone. Scientology isn't attacking people for no apparent reason. These are invented statements.

Leah Remini, Mike Rinder and Tony Ortega are all attacking Scientology. They frame the Church on "fair game" because the Church is speaking out against the discrimination and hatred.

Spreading facts about Leah and her cult followers is not "fair game" (a policy that was in the Church that has been misunderstood and was canceled thirty years ago). These people dislike how Scientology is countering their statements.

"It literally consists of if it harms Scientology it's good, if it helps Scientology it's evil. Period.

"And you know, this is, this is – the way Mike Rinder's put it, he's literally put out on a podcast that Scientology is fair game and that you may and can do anything you want against Scientology and get away with it. Literally promoting that idea." - Mark Rathbun

Leah and Mike are applying this. They use this. This is their statement regarding their attacks against Scientology.

The only statements the Church of Scientology has made are those of fact, honesty and true exposure of crimes. If Mike and Leah think that these statements arc "attacking" them, they're delusional.

Mike and Leah have stated fallacies about the statements released about them. This is presenting them as lunatics. How? They are stating that the truth is attacking them. If the truth was attacking them, wouldn't they think twice about spewing lies?

Their statements don't add up. They never will. You can waste your time thinking with it; it'll just amount to wasted time.

I hope that the people following these slimy creatures understand that what they are dealing with is fallacies every day. It's a money scheme. It's what they "dreamed up" for living expenses.

CHAPTER 18:
STAR WITNESS

This story is one of Leah's most prized possessions because she actually brought Jennifer Lopez (her partner in crime) to the wedding of Tom Cruise. This was not because of J Lo becoming a Scientologist or being disseminated to, she was simply attending the wedding with Leah Remini.

But, being as though Jennifer is not a Scientologist and is not around the Church of Scientology, people who were at the wedding wanted to greet her and meet her. This is all quite normal actually and other celebrities and public figures were there as well, Jennifer wasn't the only one that showed up.

Being as though Leah Remini would rather spin the story, I will tell you the truth. This is something Leah is very determined not to tell as it could change what people think about her. She would no longer be seen as someone "heroic" or someone like a "warrior".

Leah Remini and Jennifer Lopez got drunk. Leah was very blatant in her obsession and admiration for David Miscavige and was practically yelling very embarrassing phrases at Mr. Miscavige and about his wife.

She stated a lie which is this "I can't believe he didn't bring his wife. That is the moment I realized that she was missing." Well, if she thought she was missing the day after the wedding, I am sure that any of the church officials at the Celebrity Center in Los Angeles, California would've been able to answer that question in a heartbeat and show her some information that could've come in handy and would've stopped her thinking that she was missing.

Mike Rinder (her posse member) actually knows that she is not missing and based on the chapter I wrote about this, you should know this too. But, she still creates drama around it because she does not want the members of the church to speak out against her in regards to her real actions at that wedding and at the Scientology events that she attended.

No, Scientology wouldn't do anything but explain to her that what she was doing was harming her reputation and that they were actually trying to help her set-up gigs and interviews to boost her career. They were no stranger to Leah Remini, her career, and her family matters. Leah would talk to counselors about it all.

It was actually what she intended to do and it actually felt like she was becoming a Scientologist for real and was actually finding Scientology to help improve her life and her success stories and her actions afterwards would prove it for a short period.

The Church of Scientology has literally tried everything for Leah and to try to aid Leah in becoming a better person. She is very rude and she is very dramatic about things. She is never actually about the truth and is always about the money and the fame.

So, the next time you hear about Jennifer Lopez or Leah Remini's other tales of celebrities and Scientologists "trying to recruit them" just know, all Scientologists really do is have manners and greet those who they have seen and those they haven't seen. Some choose to give more attention to those that they don't see a lot of and others tend to give the same attention to both. That is solely up to them.

Remember, Scientology is not a closed group. It isn't some secret club that you are required to receive an invite into to find out more or attend an event. Scientologists are very friendly and very inviting and they really have no other agenda but to help you be who you want and be your friend. If you don't like the agenda that they have, don't come anywhere near the Churches of Scientology otherwise you will have a lot of conversations, smiling faces, caring attitudes, and very positive outlooks on the world at large afterwards.

The association with Jennifer Lopez and Leah Remini has definitely affected Leah's friendships even before she was expelled from the Church of Scientology.

Here is one example from a former friend:

> **"But it definitely hit me in 2008 at her sister's wedding. I was eight months pregnant and I was waddling in to go pee as very pregnant people do. And I opened the door to the lobby which is where we had entered and she looked right at me and said to somebody to her side 'I thought we closed this door to the public.' And I was like Oh! Oh, your friend, the 8-month pregnant person has to go pee and that's… that's where you're at. And I definitely, that was it for me. I was like 'Got it. I see where she's at now.'**

And it definitely started I think when she became friends with Jennifer Lopez, like she definitely started becoming very self-important. There were so many times when…like one of our best friends sent out an email like 'Hey, let's go to Disneyland for my birthday.' And there's like 10 of us on the e-mail and they're all pretty—everyone knew each other and a pretty trusted group. And she had a real problem that she wasn't blind copied on it. It's like this is Disneyland we're talking about, like to your friends, and you want to be blind copied? So there's

little clues that this, there were things that were not quite right. And her feeling very important, I think falsely."
- Julianne W.

Julianne was the friend that Leah looked upon to get away from her dark side. This, Julianne and Leah had reality with. They were very close.

CHAPTER 19:
PROPAGANDA ARMS

"They (Remini, Rinder, Ortega) deny any benefit…
of Scientology."
- Mark Rathbun

The claim is plausible for a few reasons, with the first being they really didn't participate much in the services of the religion. Some apostates worked for the church before being thrown out, and some public people participate in the social events of the church, but neither actually take advantage of the courses, the research, nor the other services that actually change people's lives for the better.

On the other hand, there is a type of person that's so wrapped up with their lies and own personal issues they just don't have the ability to change and become better until they look deep and realize they are not living happy lives.

Despite the above, you can see that Leah did benefit from Scientology from many earlier statements and interviews. She uses the statement as a witch hunt to the point of denial. Leah Remini, Mike Rinder and Tony Ortega go after the successfulness of Scientology. Their intention is to deny all prosperity.

Leah is playing the tabloids and the media like a violin. She is making it so that Scientologists are hunted down. This is like a remake of the Salem Witch Trials.

If you watch her interviews on tonight shows, you'll find that she never mentions her successes in Scientology, the benefits of Scientology, how Scientology is expanding and other factual data.

Leah entirely speaks about the information that has been programmed into her. She is the Anti-Scientology Cult's spokesperson and cannot say anything pro-Scientology. If she did, she'd probably lose funding, attention and be extorted.

> **"Their (Remini, Ortega and Rinder) narrative can be summed up very simply as, Scientology is a group of people who have no substance."**
> - Mark Rathbun

Rathbun's statement in reality makes sense. This statement is more honest than anything Leah has ever stated.

Remini, Rinder and Ortega's job is to disregard that Scientology is a philosophy that has millions of written words, thousands of hours of recorded lectures and precise techniques to employ to bring about an improved individual. This is the complete act of denial.

> **"That narrative that they tell is precisely a description of themselves. There is literally no philosophy. It is literally an anarchy of ideas. There's no solutions."**
> - Mark Rathbun

The narrative that Leah Remini and her posse are pushing is precisely what they are themselves. They are deflecting it onto Scientology. They have no substance. They don't even have a foundation.

These guys just sit around and formulate stories about Scientology. It is their job. This is what they have going for them.

> **"There is only ostracizing, marginalizing and attacking Scientologists. It's us versus them. That's the only basis upon which the group exists."**

- Mark Rathbun

I don't see truth anywhere in their claims of "exposing Scientology", "exposing the truth" or "we won't end until there's justice". I see hatred and I see a blatant agenda to attack Scientologists.

This is exactly what I've been stating, among other Scientologists and non-Scientologists. They aren't "exposing" anything; they're attacking Scientology and Scientologists.

Tony Ortega is mentioned rarely. It would really be a waste of time to reference him. He is just a wannabe blogger that was involved with Backpage.com and wrote hate articles about the Church of Scientology as a "journalist" for the Village Voice.

Mike Rinder is Leah's right-hand man. He is there with his pockets open for money. He is all about investing in lawsuits, giving people pseudo counseling and agreeing with stupid lines Leah and Tony devise about Scientology and Scientologists.

Leah, Mike and Tony have nowhere else to go in life. Their sole job is to attack Scientology and Scientologists. This is a very sad job because eventually people will come around and ignore the insanity.

CHAPTER 20: THE SKY ISN'T FALLING

For many, the apostates of a religion aren't of any interest to the members of that religion. Why is that? It doesn't take a rocket scientist to find this out and find out the actual reason why.

Here is a quote from Lonnie D. Kliever, Ph. D., Professor of Religious Studies from the property, *The Reliability of Apostate Testimony About New Religious Movements*:

"I am convinced by reason of my own professional training and scholarly research...

"that the apostate should not be accepted uncritically by the mass media, the scholarly community, the legal system, or governmental agencies as a reliable source of information about new religious movements. The apostate must always be regarded as an individual who is predisposed to render a biased account of the religious beliefs and practices of his or her former religious associations and activities."

Leah tries to paint a picture that Scientology is failing, that it is shrinking in some way, and that its members are not in the numbers that they are stated. She is in-charge of every single invented story that is pushed out of the hate factory and thus backs every single one of these claims.

This statement of expansion is found easily according to the Scientology website:

> **"During this era of rapid expansion, Church premises increased from 4.5 million square feet in 2003 to over 12 million today—more than doubling the Church's footprint around the world. Over 2.5 million square feet of renovations were completed in the past five years."**

What Leah doesn't know is this: Scientology is actually a religious movement. It is not a solid religious organization where it has churches that take memberships only and don't allow people to use their principles and such to better themselves without becoming part of the membership. That is really the truth about the religious structure.

> **"Scientology has probably been the most successful of the 20th century new religions. The first decade you measured in one church here, one new country where Scientology has been opened up to. But the closer you get to the present, the faster that growth has proceeded, both in terms of the number of new countries that have been opened to Scientology, and number of individual churches and centers that have opened, and the number of languages in which Scientology teachings have become available."**
> - Dr. J. Gordon Melton, Distinguished Professor of American Religious History of Baylor University —Institute for Studies in Religion

Scientology is a religious movement that is very fluid. It has a unique structure and it is very organized in this sense as it actually has stable management organizations and policies to keep the religion operating in this fashion.

> **"The Church of Scientology is formed into an ecclesiastical structure which unifies and aligns a multitude of diverse**

religious activities, including not only ministering Scientology religious services and practices, but proselytization, ecclesiastical management, relay of communication, production of dissemination materials and many other functions. Thus the Scientology religious community is united both by common beliefs and practices and an organizational form uniquely suited to its religious mission."
- Scientology

The principles are reaching people from all over the world, from every single religion, and even people who live different lifestyles and work different jobs. It is being applied constantly.

Now, looking at this data and knowing that Scientology is *not* shrinking and knowing that it *is* growing due to the amount of new people finding out the principles that they can use to better their lives, don't you feel a little confused?

Well, I wouldn't doubt your confusion whatsoever. Listening to Leah is confusing enough and now you have just been hit with contrary facts which clearly outline the real agenda. But, hopefully, this will help solve the other confusion.

There are new Churches of Scientology opening around the world to help show more people principles they can use in their lives without being "pen and paper" members. They can just use these principles to get better and to be successful in their lives. That is all the churches are for in actuality.

"I enjoy Scientology. Why? Because it is something that helps me in my life and I am not even a Scientologist. That is why I enjoy it so much. I am not religious but I enjoy applying Scientology."
- Carol, Writer

Then we have the Scientologists who attend services and they go to most of the religious gatherings. These people call themselves Scientologists, they come from different faiths, *and* they also help others in their lives using Scientology's principles. That is how simple it is to be a Scientologist.

"I can't imagine life without Scientology. There's a feeling of real expansion and I've been looking for this for a very long time. I looked at different spiritual things and I wanted to find out how to do it, how to get there. That's what I found in Scientology."
- Henry, Musician

As you can see, there are many people that state from actual research and not assumptions. Scientology is expanding. Scientology is making it as a fast new religious movement.

You'll find a Church of Scientology in every major city that religion is accepted. If there isn't one there, one is in preparation or planning stages.

CHAPTER 21: DISCONNECTION

L eah has been broadcasting that Scientology disconnects families. She has been providing this narrative for a while. According to Leah's former show she is obsessed with talking about disconnection in Scientology and how it tears families apart.

An example would be if you have an alcoholic uncle who is mean, steals from you, constantly gets into trouble with the law, and generally rejects any of your help. If you should decide that person is no longer worth your time, you might say that's it and just break off any contact with him. This is an example of what they term a horrible 'disconnection'.

Scientology doesn't interfere with families, relationships or marriages. Scientology as an entity doesn't involve itself in personal affairs. The purpose of the church is to allow people to look at situations and life in a safe and free manner that lets them come to any conclusion that is best for them and doesn't hurt others.

Leah Remini and Mike Rinder have provided this narrative to their viewers. Disconnection isn't enforced. Disconnection isn't an official policy in the Church.

"There is no Scientology Disconnection policy that requires Church members to disconnect from anyone, let alone family and friends who simply have different beliefs. To the contrary, the moral code of Scientology mandates that Scientologists respect the religious beliefs of others. The Church encourages excellent family relationships, Scientologists or not, and family relations routinely improve with Scientology because the Scientologist learns how to increase communication and resolve any problems that may have previously existed."
- Church of Scientology International

Maybe you have someone in your life that is constantly negative and won't respect any of your wishes. That's the same thing, as it doesn't just have to be about religion.

Disconnection isn't as bad as it sounds. Leah and Mike are making it seem like it is forced upon them. It is solely up to the individual Scientologist. Wherever the Scientologist is in Scientology, it is solely their decision.

This is what L. Ron Hubbard states about it:

"The term handle most commonly means to smooth out a situation with another person by applying the technology of communication.

"The term disconnection is defined as a self-determined decision made by an individual that he is not going to be connected to another. It is a severing of a communication line.

"The basic principle of 'handle or disconnect' exists in any group and ours is no different.

"It is much like trying to deal with a criminal. If he will not handle, the society resorts to the only other solution: It 'disconnects' the criminal from society. In other words, they remove the guy from society and put him in a prison because he won't handle his problem or otherwise

cease to commit criminal acts against others."

A person is simply exercising their right to communicate. That is what they are practicing, as Mr. Hubbard further states:

"If one has the right to communicate, then one must also have the right to not receive communication from another. It is this latter corollary of the right to communicate that gives us our right to privacy."

People have rights. Scientologists have rights. Their rights aren't to be taken away by those who wish to cause them harm.

L. Ron Hubbard wrote this in accordance with other religions' references involving disconnection.

Scientologists aren't to disconnect from family members, friends and co-workers because of their religious belief and practice. This is contrary to the belief of Scientology: *Respect the Religious Beliefs of Others*.

It isn't unusual to allow someone the right to not communicate with someone who is causing them trouble. I wouldn't want to be forced to communicate with someone who harassed me every day.

How about the wife that is being beaten on a daily basis, should this wife continue to get beaten up? Should she continue to be involved with this person despite that she is being beaten?

Dr. Benjamin J. Hubbard, Professor Emeritus of Comparative Religions at California State University, Fullerton, looked at Scientology's right to disconnection and compared it with other religions' practices. This is what Dr. Hubbard found:

"On the basis of my comparison of the practice of disconnection within Scientology to similar practices within other contemporary faiths, I see no reason to single out this religion as espousing unique or bizarre rituals for separating a disruptive person from the community of believers."

"Such a community is held together by common agreements on right and wrong conduct and methods for preserving its integrity. All faiths have this attribute in one form or another. The policies of the Church of Scientology in this regard are by no means unique and fall well within the spectrum of acceptable conduct."

My acknowledgment goes to Dr. Hubbard for comparing it, coming out with a statement and sharing the truth.

The next point is the comparison of other religions' practices of "Disconnection".

Here is a statement from the Church of Scientology International regarding "Disconnection" compared to other religions:

"Scientologists practice disconnection as a last resort after all other avenues of reconciliation have been exhausted. In Scientology, inclusion rather than exclusion is preferred. As with other faiths, the Scientology practice does not involve disconnecting from people because they have different beliefs. Scientologists live and work on a daily basis with Jews, Protestants, Catholics, Mormons, Muslims, Hindus, Buddhists and atheists. Scientologists are taught to respect the religious beliefs of others."

Jehovah's Witnesses

Jehovah's Witnesses use a practice known as disfelowshipping. The shunned person is not to be acknowledged in everyday life or at their Sunday Services.

"We do not automatically disfellowship someone who commits a serious sin. If, however, a baptized Witness makes a practice of breaking the Bible's moral code and does not repent, he or she will be shunned or disfellowshipped. The Bible clearly states: ""Remove

the wicked man from among yourselves.""
—1 Corinthians 5:13.

What of a man who is disfellowshipped but whose
wife and children are still Jehovah's Witnesses? The
religious ties he had with his family change, but
blood ties remain. The marriage relationship and
normal family affections and dealings continue.

Disfellowshipped individuals may attend our religious
services. If they wish, they may also receive spiritual
counsel from the congregation elders. The goal is to
help each individual once more to qualify to be one of
Jehovah's Witnesses. Disfellowshipped people who
reject improper conduct and demonstrate a sincere
desire to live by the Bible's standards are always welcome
to become members of the congregation again."
- JW.org

Mormonism

"A parade of anti-Christs, anti-Mormons, and apostate
groups have appeared on the scene. Many are still among us
and have released new floods of lies and false accusations.
These faith-killers and testimony-thieves use personal
contacts, the printed word, electronic media, and other
means of communication to sow doubts and to disturb
the peace of true believers...Avoid those who would
tear down your faith. Faith-killers are to be shunned.
The seeds which they planted in the minds and hearts
of men grow like cancer and eat away the Spirit."
- "Opposition to the Work of God," Carlos E. Asay
- General Conference, October 1981.

Judaism

"The Talmud forbids coming within six feet of a person
who has been excommunicated. During medieval times, the

> laws of excommunication could be extended to the family of the person who was convicted of a crime. Additionally, there existed a weaker form of excommunication, called niddui that was applied for only thirty days. Even the threat of being excommunicated was employed to guarantee the acceptance and submission of the laws."
> - Jewish Virtual Library

I've had to disconnect many former co-workers of mine. Why? These individuals had found out that I'm a Scientologist. Instead of asking me questions about it, respecting my beliefs and practices and treating me like a human being – they went on witch hunts.

I was attacked through hate-mail, harassment, invalidation, spreading false information and even got to the point of contacting my family members and my girlfriend to spread gossip. This was complete hell. I regret ever working with them.

I had attempted to handle the individuals, they were very two-faced. These specific co-workers would act like everything I was communicating was agreeable and then slam me to their friends and managers behind closed doors.

I would write communications to corporate. These communications would be ignored due to the information these co-workers spread to corporate about me. These individuals stated this "Ryan is unethical, unprofessional, dishonest and is under investigation". This stated that I was a red-flag, but in actuality, they were the red-flag.

After dealing with this for too long without any correction, I had given my two-week notice. That was the end. I had deleted contact information, told them not to contact me and if they found my information from somewhere and attempted to – I wouldn't answer.

They haven't since. My life has been better than ever before. I am volunteering with my Church, helping my friends, studying sales with an online university and personally improving.

I could go on with more examples. Religions practice disconnection, excommunication and shunning. That is simply what their members practice as their right.

Scientology is no different than other religions with their right to disconnection. There is nothing illegal about choosing to disassociate yourself with someone who suppresses you, harasses you and doesn't support your religious beliefs and practices. This is even after everything you've tried to mend the situation.

Leah and Mike need to stop. This isn't a problem. The people who are stating lies about it are displaying the reason why they were disconnected from. I wouldn't associate myself with any of those who are connected to Leah Remini and Mike Rinder.

CHAPTER 22: SERVICES, EXPANSION AND SCIENTOLOGY TODAY

Y ou're now about to be introduced to the Scientology Leah doesn't know and will not be able to tell you about. Everything she talks about may have happened sometime in the past, but first it's twisted for ratings impact, and second it's from many years ago when the religion was still forming and I'm sure some crazy people were working at the Church and causing legitimate problems.

This is going to be the polar opposite of what you've heard and so you will have to ensure that you are ready to hear how it has changed and how it has worked to improve every inch of the religion.

Here is but a glimpse of Scientology today and all that's happened since she 'escaped' (meaning expelled from) the Church. This is by no means to replace seeing it for your own eyes and experiencing it for yourself.

Golden Age of Knowledge

It all starts with the Golden *Age of Knowledge* which culminated close to 30 years of research, archiving, and the correction of *ALL* written and recorded scriptures by the Founder. This meant dedicating over millions of hours, miles, and even consisting of hundreds of people to make an impact on this project. This was led by David Miscavige (Leader of Scientology) and was completed in 2010.

> **"We are not speaking of 'corrected' manuscripts,**
> **not 'newly verified' manuscripts. And definitely**
> **not just 'repackaged.' What we are speaking of**
> **is 100 percent unadulterated SOURCE."**
> - David Miscavige, Leader of Scientology

Mr. Hubbard is the source of the information and over the years it was found people made changes to his research. Some of it by accident as in the case of typists and dictation transcription errors, and some much more sinister that changed the materials so they would not generate the positive results that Hubbard intended.

Fixing this problem meant that all recorded lectures and written words were confirmed all the way back to original handwritten pages and the actual reel to reel audio recordings that were 100% by the Founder. This was started because Mr. Miscavige found actual alterations in the written words, transcripts, and even his policy letters. People had also come into the religion and tried to alter what the Founder had stated to cause people harm using Scientology principles and thus causing people to distrust and brush off the principles as mistakenly useless. BUT, they were not useless and they had only been altered by some people with the intent of infiltrating Scientology to start a "demise" or "downfall".

Mr. Miscavige announced not only a decade of milestone

accomplishments, but the most monumental achievement in the history of the religion—completion of the 25-year program to recover, verify and restore the Scripture of the Scientology religion. The quarter-century endeavor that involved some 2 million man-hours to recover and make fully accessible all written and spoken words of L. Ron Hubbard constituted "the ultimate guarantee for the permanency of Scientology itself," said Mr. Miscavige.

L. Ron Hubbard initiated the program in 1984 to provide Scientologists the full legacy of his 50 years of research and discovery into the mind, spirit and life. What followed were years of locating all manuscripts and recordings in cities where Mr. Hubbard wrote and lectured, and the verification and restoration of those materials.
- Church of Scientology

David Miscavige released millions of written words and thousands of recorded lectures from what are known now as *The Basics, The Congresses, The Advanced Clinical Courses, and The Classics.* Scientologists and non-Scientologists are now able to purchase these materials from the Church and from other booksellers around the globe. It was a monumental accomplishment that has caused over 200 million copies to be distributed since the release of *Golden Age of Knowledge* in the Church.

"These tapes provide the only existing running day-to-day, week-to-week record of the progress of research in Dianetics and Scientology. They were blazing a trail from total ignorance of the subject to today. Man knew nothing about the mind when it began and we are where we are today. And these tapes were the milestones on the way out."
- David Miscavige, Leader of Scientology

The core beliefs of the Scientology religion are publicly available to anyone. These are contained in any one of the 18 Basic books and accompanying 280 lectures by L. Ron

Hubbard available in every Church and mission of Scientology worldwide, as well as public libraries internationally. In these references, Mr. Hubbard writes and speaks on the origins of the universe, the questions of Man's relation to the Supreme Being as well as the Creation Theory (The Factors) of the Scientology religion.
- Church of Scientology

If you thought that was all, well you have missed the point of monumental. That word does not necessarily describe anything about finding lost words, finding prevented words, and finding the exact words that the Founder used to describe exact processes in the Church, exact policies in the Church, and to produce something so exact that nobody could penetrate it with any infiltration. This ended up being one of the many monumental moments in Scientology.

Ideal Organizations

The next phase that really got underway after Leah's departure is the *Church of Scientology Ideal Organizations* project started in 2003. This project picked up while *Golden Age of Knowledge* was being worked on and released. This project meant that "Ideal" Churches of Scientology would meet the standards of what the Founder stated about Scientology, Dianetics, and their supported humanitarian efforts.

Mr. Miscavige is the driving force of a movement now spanning the globe with Ideal Churches of Scientology. He set the direction for the acquisition, design and planning of new Churches and in consequence, the horizons of Scientology are filled with scores of new Churches in the making for the second decade of the century.
- Church of Scientology

These Churches would embody the ideal scene of Scientology

principles and would be the entrance point for answers for the general public and for Scientologists, internationally.

An Ideal Org is a Church configured to provide the full services of the Scientology religion to its parishioners and to the community. "Ideal" encompasses both the physical facilities and the types of services ministered to parishioners and the community. These Churches house extensive public information multimedia displays describing all aspects of Dianetics and Scientology, Founder L. Ron Hubbard, and the Church's social betterment and community outreach programs. - Church of Scientology

While *Golden Age of Knowledge* was being worked on there were Churches of this category opening in Johannesburg, South Africa; San Francisco, California; Madrid, Spain and a few more. The Church was absolutely focused on both projects but, one had more attention at the time.

David Miscavige took all of the Church's attention and put it on this *Church of Scientology Ideal Organizations* project which was now in coordination with the Church's *Building Expansion Unit* and *Church of Scientology International* fully. David Miscavige personally opened organizations from Belgium, United Kingdom, Germany, Italy, United States, Russia, Canada, Mexico, Japan, and many other countries. This project is still happening today and is becoming one of the biggest expansion projects in religious history.

Church premises increased from 5.6 million square feet in 2004 to over 11.5 million by the beginning of the new decade, with a million and a half square feet of renovations completed in the last two years and over a quarter of a million square feet now under construction.
- Church of Scientology

David Miscavige has announced the completion of a few more Ideal Churches of Scientology or "Ideal Orgs". These Ideal Orgs are in Columbus, Ohio; Kansas City, Missouri; Austin, Texas; Santa Barbara, California; and many other major cities across Earth.

The finished Ideal Orgs are in Johannesburg, South Africa; San Francisco, CA; Dallas, TX; Los Angeles, CA; Los Gatos, CA; Silicon Valley, CA; San Fernando Valley, CA; Stevens Creek, CA; Mountain View, CA; Inglewood, CA; Sacramento, CA; Phoenix, AZ; Las Vegas, NV; Pretoria, South Africa; Madrid, Spain; Padova, Italy; Rome, Italy; Milan, Italy; Moscow, Russia; Kirche, Germany; Brussels, Belgium; Copenhagen, Denmark, and about 70 more.

Since 2003 over fifty Ideal Churches have arisen across the planet, including those in the world's cultural capitals— the National Church of Scientology of Spain in Madrid's Neighborhood of Letters; the Church of Scientology of New York, just off Times Square; the Church of Scientology of San Francisco, California, in the original historic Transamerica Building; the Church of Scientology of London, England, located in the epicenter of the city; the Church of Scientology of Berlin, Germany, near the Brandenburg Gate; and the Church of Scientology of Moscow, Russia, located just a short distance from the Kremlin and Red Square. Over thirty new Churches have been opened just since 2009.
- Church of Scientology

Scientology will have completed its Western United States goal after Ventura, California (or Santa Barbara, CA) is complete. This is a Church that will meet the massive expansion project for the current target and plan for Scientology Ideal Organizations on this side of the country. The Church will now focus on the Eastern United States with their Ideal Organizations underway right now.

Another 60 Churches are in design, planning or construction phases, including over a quarter of a million square feet under construction.

- Church of Scientology

Expansion Fundraising

Along with the efforts to re-create the Church to the Founder's expectations and fuel the expansion needed to make Scientology available around the world, fundraising efforts were started much like any Church does to raise money. The fundraising on these projects is solely done as a charitable effort and parishioners willingly give these amounts necessary to open these amazingly standard organizations.

Scientology does not have hundreds of years of accumulated wealth and property like other religions; it must make its way in the world according to the economics of today's society. When one considers the cost of ministering even one hour of auditing, requiring extensively trained auditors, not to mention overhead costs of maintaining Church premises, the necessity of donations becomes clear.
- Church of Scientology ·

I have been to numerous fundraising gatherings and they are so uplifting and so motivational that I have to double check to see if that is actually the amount of support we gathered. There are surprise donations and there are those that people actually work for throughout their life's work and their monthly paycheck.

When attending an event involving donations towards Scientology "Ideal" Organizations, you are not required to donate. You can attend for the information and mingle with your friends.

The Church staff and officials are only there to ensure that the parishioner is actually well oriented to the purpose of the donation and to help them finish the process with the invoicing so that their contribution is completed (as they have requested).

I may not have a lot of money, but I have done quite a bit as young as I am. When I started working in the Church I was not wealthy, and I was a young person. I was actually doing it because I knew that it was something that I wanted to do and support when I was older. I was *completely* correct. I definitely want to continue to support Scientology and Scientologists and ensure that people are helped regardless of their religion, race, background, gender, and any other classification.

Being a Scientologist, you are not required to donate to any of the efforts or services. These donations are just used like any other religion, but they are used <u>wisely</u> and they are actually used to provide support to the supported humanitarian efforts and also provide free materials to those who are interested in finding out more about Scientology.

You'll also find the donations are used very effectively and buy more per dollar in value than many other charitable causes. As an example, many donations campaigns use 100% of the funds for the actual project, while often other organizations will take a portion and spend it on 'overhead' and other 'administrative' expenses. The Church will often raise $10,000 for a drug prevention program, and all of that money actually goes to delivering that program fully.

The Church selected the donation system as its primary method of funding because it is the most equitable. Those who most use Church facilities should be the ones who contribute most to its maintenance. Of course, no donation is expected from members who are at the Church to participate in a variety of other individual and congregational services which take place seven days a week—including participation in Group Processing, listening to tape plays of L. Ron Hubbard's lectures, reading scriptural works in the Church library, meeting with fellow parishioners, receiving counseling from the Chaplain or attending Sunday services,

weddings, christenings and funerals.
- Church of Scientology

When you look at one of the most recent Churches of Scientology, they are put there with the Scientologists' support. The Haters claim this is robbery and coercion and a crime against God, but as usual the facts show this is not unheard of in other religions. Many religions fundraise to expand, support others, and provide free information to another by collecting support from their parishioners for spreading message farther and ultimately across the globe.

The Church of Scientology supports anyone from anywhere as long as they are providing help in a pro-survival way. That is actually what we are looking at as Scientologists. As long as you are helping, you have earned our support.

"The Scientologists let me use their Chapel for my drug prevention seminar. I was looking for a venue for my congregation and I and I found it!"
- Tim, Drug Educator

Fundraising is not a main part in the religion though; it is not something that they focus on all of the time. Fundraising and donations are only a section of the religion.

Some people have a lot of attention on money in their lives and thus need to think about money exclusively in Scientology or every other religion for that matter – that is completely not true. The religion does not require a Scientologist or any Church official to think about donations all of the time.

Some churches have a system of tithes. Others require members to pay for pew rentals, religious ceremonies and services. In the Church of Scientology, parishioners make donations for auditing or training they wish to receive. These contributions are the primary source of financial support for the Church and fund all Church-sponsored religious and social

betterment activities. Scientologists are not required to tithe or make other donations.
- Church of Scientology

This goes into the policies of L. Ron Hubbard and for those writings and recorded lectures, you'll have to get those from an official of the nearest Church of Scientology or at least have your questions answered.

The International Association of Scientologists

There is an organization that you may know or have heard of called *The International Association of Scientologists;* this organization is the membership entity of Scientology. The reach of the IAS throughout the world to help people and improve conditions around the world is amazing.

Membership dues, around $200 annually for a voluntary, annual subscription go exclusively to their supported humanitarian efforts, their advanced organizations, and other such projects that exclusively are designed to help improve the community and also that are designed to protect Scientology and Scientologists all over the world. That is the purpose of this entity. I would urge you to find out more about this organization and see what it has sponsored with the support of Scientologists and even those who are not Scientologists.

The International Association of Scientologists (IAS) is an unincorporated membership organization open to all Scientologists from all nations.

The IAS was formed in 1984 at a time when the religious freedom of Scientologists was imperiled. Delegates from Scientology Churches world over assembled at Saint Hill Manor (L. Ron Hubbard's home from 1959 to 1966) in recognition of the need to unite all Scientologists

as an international body. To confirm their dedication toward the Aims of Scientology, those first IAS delegates formulated and signed The Pledge to Mankind.

The purpose of the IAS is: "To unite, advance, support and protect the Scientology religion and Scientologists in all parts of the world so as to achieve the Aims of Scientology as originated by L. Ron Hubbard."
- Church of Scientology

Learn more at: https://www.iasmembership.org/

Golden Age of Tech Phase II

As many projects unfolded after and without Leah, Mr. Miscavige wanted to ensure that after the Golden *Age of Knowledge* was accomplished and the *Ideal Organizations Project* was being executed, that the technology and application of Scientology and Dianetics were as exact as what the Founder intended.

Mr. Miscavige executed a project that would entail hundreds of thousands of hours and many years of complete research, discovery, and verification of the writings that were released and compares them to the original writings of the Founder. This wasn't going to be easy.

This project involved millions of hours, hundreds of people and very precise techniques. Restoring and verifying all policies and services of the Church took a lot of effort.

In November 2013 it was completed it spanned more than every single inch of Scientology services on *The Bridge to Total Freedom* being released newly and having been verified and made available *exactly* and *100%* of what the Founder would've wanted. Mr. Miscavige released this with the monumental and landmark accomplishment of training more than 1,000 individual counselors and supervisors for all of the Churches of Scientology around the globe.

This was the largest training program in Scientology history. It culminated over 1,000 Course Supervisors and Spiritual Counselors from every Church of Scientology.

This was something that wasn't predicted in the history of Scientology and religion. That is something that you cannot do with Christianity as Jesus Christ is not around any longer and the Bible has been changed numerous times that some original writings have either been removed or they are just altered completely.

The Golden Age of Tech Phase II followed on the heels of the Golden Age of Knowledge—an evolution that involved nothing less than the full audio restoration of all 3,000 LRH lectures and the recovery of the complete, day-by-day path of his discovery and development.
- Church of Scientology

When Mr. Miscavige completed the *Golden Age of Technology Phase Two,* which is what all of the training, discoveries, research, restoration, and other forms of verification for over three decades, this was jaw-dropping for those secretly inside the Scientology religion to infiltrate it. At this moment in time, they already knew their mission was doomed. Their mission was completely obliterated and their lies would be wiped out just from the amount of people achieving the gains from Scientology and being able to look for themselves, without alterations.

These are some of the statements from those who attended the release event for *Golden Age of Technology Phase II*:

"This does not affect just one little thing. But EVERYTHING! It's like taking the Golden Age of Tech, plus Golden Age of Knowledge and multiplying this by 10 times, and you

might then get some concept of what's going on. I couldn't even count how many times I had to pick my jaw up off the floor. It was crazy! I was totally flabbergasted."
—K.C.

"The Golden Age of Tech Phase II really inaugurates an explosive stage of Scientology growth. It is power-packed and it is so distilled that it is going to release a tremendous wave of liberation on the planet. I am truly in awe of how much work was put into the research of all of the Bridge from the top to the bottom. This is so great and I am very excited for the future—my children and their children. It is impossible to overestimate the impact of Golden Age of Tech Phase II!"
—T.W.

"My son is one of the people that trained on Golden Age of Tech Phase II. Now I know that all the orgs planet-wide will have this technology. Standard Tech will be delivered standardly with Keeping Scientology Working fully in. It's all laid out as LRH wanted it to be. It is happening now. What this means is that we are ready to deliver to all Scientologists with open arms and the way it's supposed to be. The way this is laid out makes you really comprehend the magnitude of what is going to happen."
— P.A.

"I really admire all the work that has been done. Everything was taken into account, every little thing! Mr. David Miscavige has given us everything we have been waiting for and dreaming about. I am so filled with emotion! Hurray."
— G.R.

The Flag Building

Leah pretended to be a Scientologist in the 1990's and everything you've read thus far show what took place after her being run out. Another huge accomplishment is what is known in Scientology as *The Flag Building*. This is a massive building that stands as the Scientology Religious and Spiritual Cathedral which is to serve as the place where international parishioners can come to experience the advanced levels of Scientology services and to experience an environment where Scientologists from around the globe come to continue services with their religious path.

The latest phase of expansion came to fruition on November 17, 2013 when the monumental Flag Building opened its doors. More than 10,000 Scientologists gathered for the dedication ceremony, which was led by Mr. David Miscavige. The building is an architectural triumph, standing 377,000 square feet and occupying a full city block.
- Church of Scientology

This project was three decades in the making. This took millions of dollars, thousands of hours, and international support from parishioners in other such ways as well. It was a project that had been planned since Mr. Miscavige was given the position to be the Leader of Scientology by the Founder.

"My fellow Scientologists, the best on the planet now awaits you. For the doors to your Flag Building are open and I officially invite you to cross the threshold to a whole new world."
—Mr. David Miscavige,
Chairman of the Board Religious Technology Center

This project was something that even my family donated to, though we didn't donate much, we donated a fair chunk and helped the project's forward motion throughout the future. As it is now open, I can share with you some amazing stories from those who helped put this building here.

I was speaking to one of my friends who works for a Fortune 500 company now but, before he was working for a fast food chain making minimum wage, he was making a decent income and saving some money on the side. He wasn't doing that well but he was making ends meet.

One day I told him about this project. I told him that the Flag Building is underway and that it is closer than ever before. He was thrilled and he actually brightened up when he heard this because his parents donated to it in the early 2000's and has been hearing a bit since.

He and I kept in touch for a month or two about this project off and on, we just kept thinking of ways we could support it. He was working and I was working and we just kept dreaming up ways of helping. But, out of the blue he calls me; he called me to tell me this:

> **"Ryan, I have to tell you what I am going to do to back up this project. We, as Scientologists, need this facility. We need this as our international hub and I am barely even able to start my service at my local Org. I would love for a chance to rejuvenate my friends and I.**

> **"But, here is what I will do. I am going to do a hefty donation to the Flag Building in hopes that it will open very soon. I can barely hold my bills together but, I am going to do this for the religion and for you and I, as Scientologists.**

> **"I know that my parents will be proud when I tell them. I will let you know when I do this donation and then you can follow this with something magical as well."**

After this call, he had donated a massive amount that I didn't know that he had. He had done this all through his own efforts and his own determination. It was invoiced and donated to the project's fund.

> **"The building is absolutely awesome. It is our cathedral. It takes function and gives it its ideal form. It represents exactly what the Scientology staff does**

with the technology. When it comes to architecture,
this building could not get better. It's heaven."
—M.B.

Funny enough, his donation was one of the last donations to go into the project because it was finally opening and it was opening five months from that point and he didn't even know yet. He contributed to one of the biggest projects in Scientology history, thus far.

"I've been in Scientology since 1973. This is a milestone in
the expansion of Scientology, which is hugely significant
for me, my family and Mankind. This will truly impact
our future. Thank you a million times to COB RTC!"
—P.B.

"The details and just exactly how everything
is thought through stand out the most. The Flag
Building really does mean a whole new world. It is
a game changer. Nothing can stop us now."
—S.B.

Now, I won't go too far into these landmark moments for Scientology because I know that you could go to the websites of Scientology's and find out more information and so forth, but I like giving people even more information to where they are swimming in data that they can investigate for themselves.

All began with the launch of the crusade in the name of Ideal
Organizations, now spanning five continents. What followed
was the recovery of the very foundation of Scientology and
the Golden Age of Knowledge; next, the recovery of every L.
Ron Hubbard Introductory Route at the entrance gates to the
Bridge; and then, nothing less than the recovery of the Bridge
itself from bottom to top, ushering in our Golden Age of Tech
Phase II.
- Church of Scientology

CHAPTER 23:
SCIENTOLOGY
AUDITING

Okay the word auditing is something people hear and generally they have no idea what it means. Let me define it and then explain it briefly here.

Definition of auditing: Auditing, from the Latin audire meaning "to hear or listen", is the name given to a range of Scientology procedures intended to help people become aware of their spiritual nature and more able in life. Auditing can be ministered to a group (such as at a Scientology Sunday service) or to an individual on a one-to-one basis. A person can also minister certain auditing to himself. All Scientology churches have rooms designated for auditing.

Some of the counseling services use a meter to help locate the exact upset in a person's life, something that is upsetting to them.

Definition of e-meter: *E-Meter* is a shortened term for *electropsychometer*. It is a religious artifact used as a spiritual guide in auditing. It is for use only by a Scientology minister or a Scientology minister-in-training to help the preclear locate and confront areas of spiritual upset.

People go through losses, troubles and various implications that hold them back. These are not necessarily physical problems and they're not treated with chemical solutions.

Scientology addresses these with spiritual counseling. This is simple and has exact processes. This particular counseling was researched and developed by L. Ron Hubbard.

Here is a disclaimer:

> **Scientology is not in the business of curing ailments in any traditional sense of the word. Auditing is not done to repair the body or heal anything physical, and the E-Meter cures nothing. However, in the process of becoming happier, more able and more aware as a spiritual being through auditing, illnesses that are psychosomatic in origin (meaning illnesses caused by the soul) often disappear.**

When the uninformed talk about auditing, they often refer to "curing". This is further from the factual purpose of auditing. L. Ron Hubbard didn't research and develop this technology to cure anyone of any ailments. Many people agree that when someone is in good mental condition and physically fit, the body can 'heal itself' and not develop the many ailments you see your friends and family experiencing.

> **Scientology auditing is ministered in a specific sequence which handles the major barriers people encounter when trying to achieve their goals. After receiving auditing, one will start to recognize for oneself the change, that one's outlook on life is improving and that one is becoming more able. In Scientology, a person will not be told when they have completed an auditing level—they will know for themselves, as only they can know exactly what they are experiencing. This gives them the certainty that they have attained the spiritual advances that they want to attain from each level.**

I can state that I have received Scientology auditing and it's very spiritual. It helped me improve my communication skills with my family, before auditing I wasn't doing great in communication.

**We are not making any claims for Dianetics or
Scientology. When you have experienced it,
it is you who will make the claims.**

E-Meter is a shortened term for electro-psychometer. It is a religious artifact used as a spiritual guide in auditing. It is for use only by a Scientology minister or a Scientology minister-in-training to help the person locate and confront areas of spiritual upset.

This is the statement about the E-Meter from Scientology:

**"In itself, the E-Meter does nothing. It is an electronic
instrument that measures mental state and change of
state in individuals and assists the precision and speed
of auditing. The E-Meter is not intended or effective for
the diagnosis, treatment or prevention of any disease.**

**In order to understand how the E-Meter works, it is necessary
to understand some basic Scientology concepts.**

**There are three basic parts of Man—mind, body and
thetan. The thetan is an immortal spiritual being—the
individual himself. The thetan inhabits a body and has a
mind, which is a collection of mental image pictures.**

**The pictures in the mind contain energy and mass. The
energy and force in pictures of painful or upsetting
experiences can have a harmful effect upon an individual.
This harmful energy or force is called charge.**

**When the E-Meter is operating and a person holds the meter's
electrodes, a very tiny flow of electrical energy (About
1.5 volts—less than a flashlight battery) passes down the**

wires of the E-Meter leads, through the person's body and back into the E-Meter. (The electrical flow is so small; there is no physical sensation when holding the electrodes.)

When the person thinks a thought, looks at a picture in their mind, re-experiences an incident or shifts some part of the reactive mind, they are moving and changing actual mental mass and energy. These changes in the mind influence the tiny flow of electrical energy generated by the E-Meter, causing the needle on its dial to move. The needle reactions on the E-Meter tell the auditor where the charge lies, and that it should be addressed through auditing."

I have received numerous hours of auditing. These are personal experiences for me. They address me as a spiritual being and the painful and stressful incidents in my life.

The auditing that I have received has only improved my ability to communicate, work, organize, etc. Scientology Auditors are very precise and they care about people.

A person trained and qualified to better people through auditing is called an auditor. Auditor is defined as one who listens, from the Latin audire meaning to hear or listen. An auditor is a minister or minister-in-training of the Church of Scientology.

A person receiving auditing is called a preclear —from pre (before) and "Clear," a person not yet Clear. A preclear is a person who, through auditing, is finding out more about himself and life.

You'll find people in Churches of Scientology around the world who've received Scientology Auditing. You'll find people that are training to become Scientology Auditors. You'll also find people who're just finding out about Scientology Auditing.

The straight truth is everyone on this planet could use some relief. That's all Scientology is interested in providing. If it helps you with more than relief, that is fantastic.

Leah mentions that in order to receive Scientology Auditing you have to pay money. Yes, it is a service you can buy but there is also free auditing available from the student auditors who need to practice counseling before becoming a certified Scientology Auditor.

As for the paid services there are requested donation rates for every Church of Scientology. I'll provide you with the statement from the Church:

"Scientology does not have hundreds of years of accumulated wealth and property like other religions; it must make its way in the world according to the economics of today's society. When one considers the cost of ministering even one hour of auditing, requiring extensively trained auditors, not to mention overhead costs of maintaining Church premises, the necessity of donations becomes clear."

This doesn't mean Scientology requests unreasonable donation amounts. Scientology requests what was agreed upon with the Founder's policies. The Founder's policies are based on financial estimates to continue operating all of the Church premises, staff pay, supported programs, materials and all responsibilities.

Scientology's Leader, Mr. Miscavige, is ensuring standard financial policy is followed in every Church of Scientology. He has made it possible, with the release of Golden Age of Technology Phase II, for faster progress through auditing and more affordable for the Church and for the Scientologists, all while also improving the delivery standards of the processes.

"Scientologists' donations keep the Church alive and functioning, fund its widespread social reform programs, make Scientology known to people who might otherwise never have the opportunity to avail themselves of it and help create a safe and pleasant environment for everyone."

- Church of Scientology International

This is important to all Scientologists. This is important to those relying on the Church of Scientology for their humanitarian efforts. This is very important to those who are relying on the Church premises to handle their bills and to pay their Staff.

Newly, Scientology has released a Free Scientology Center, for those who cannot afford Scientology Auditing. You can find out more through a Church of Scientology, they'll provide you with the details.

Many have asked to learn more about the auditing itself. What is it? How does it work?

Auditing uses processes—exact sets of questions asked or directions given by an auditor to help a person locate areas of spiritual distress, find out things about himself and improve his condition. Many, many different auditing processes exist and each one improves the individual's ability to confront and handle some part of his existence. When the specific objective of any one process is attained, the process is ended and another can then be used to address a different part of the person's life.

This doesn't have any relation to Psychiatry and Psychology. This doesn't deal with drugs, hypnotism, electroshock and lobotomy. Auditing is very clean and safe.

This isn't a sham, unlike other attempts at addressing a person's imperfections spiritually. You may ask: How is this validated in Scientology? How is this validated for those outside of Scientology?

"Numerous tests are used to measure the preclear's ability prior to starting an auditing program and also provide a prediction of how much auditing it may take to achieve a certain result with the preclear. When retested afterwards, the improvements he experiences personally

can be plotted on a graph, which validates his gains.

These objective measures of a person's improvement fly in the face of commonly held beliefs. Prior to Dianetics, psychiatry and psychology were adamant in their assertion that a person's ability and intelligence could not be changed. Their pronouncements were disproven in the face of study after study wherein people showed dramatic increases in both areas after auditing.

One routine test, adapted by the Church itself, is known as the Oxford Capacity Analysis (OCA) which is designed to graphically represent ten different personality traits. These rise markedly in auditing, reflecting the preclear's gains. Preclears report being calmer, more stable, more energetic and more outgoing as a direct result of auditing and scores on the OCA furnish corroborative data.

Aptitude tests are also a reliable indicator of auditing results. Improvements in aptitude test scores correlate with a decrease in propensity toward accidents. Many other tests are available that measure coordination and perceptions such as vision, hearing, color blindness, balance and so on. These functions also improve as a result of auditing.

Naturally, individual progress is variable since it is largely influenced by the preclear's dedication and the frequency of sessions. Therefore, clearly defined rates of improvement are impossible to establish and the Church makes no claims or guarantees of the gains someone will make in auditing. Church staff, however, have seen so many remarkable improvements in parishioners that they expect such results as a matter of course."
- Church of Scientology International

Scientology is good at the validation of results. I have experienced positive results. I have used aptitude, personality and IQ testing, I have found that it shows improvement. I feel the improvement before even doing the testing; the testing just backs up and confirms the feeling.

The question still remains, where does an "Auditing Session" (Counseling Session) take place? What does it include?

"A one-to-one auditing session takes place in a quiet, comfortable place where it will not be disturbed. Where auditing is ministered one-on-one usually the auditor and preclear are seated across a table or desk from one another with an E-Meter set up for the auditor's use. Before a program of auditing begins, the preclear is familiarized with the elements of auditing during a period of orientation so he knows what to expect in a session. The auditor also ensures the preclear has no distractions or upsets to prevent him from devoting his full attention to the process used in the session."
- Church of Scientology International

You've also heard Leah and Mike mention the goal of Scientology Auditing. No, it isn't what they state.

"The goal of auditing is to restore beingness and ability. This is accomplished by (1) helping the individual rid himself of any spiritual disabilities and (2) increasing individual abilities. Obviously, both are necessary for an individual to achieve his full spiritual potential. Auditing can be ministered to a group (such as at a Scientology Sunday service), by a person on his own using certain Scientology books and materials and one-to-one."
- Church of Scientology International

Many have asked, does Scientology Auditing have any relation to Psychiatry?

"Auditing is quite different from these past practices, many of which were ineffective and some, like psychiatry, which were actually harmful. In auditing one follows a precisely mapped route which leads to specific improvements and it is only the

individual being audited who says whether these have been achieved or not. The preclear determines when he has regained an ability or rid himself of a spiritual barrier to living, not anyone else. The auditor continues to minister to the preclear until the preclear knows of his own volition that he has succeeded. It is not the auditor or anyone else in Scientology who says the preclear has made a gain. The preclear himself knows. Given that the goal of auditing is rehabilitation of one's own potentials, the gains can really be determined in no other way."
- Church of Scientology International

Auditing is Scientology's fundamental practice. This is in place of worship, like other religions. Scientology is precisely focused on improving the individual's abilities and thus creating a happier and spiritually free life.

No more thinking about taking drugs, feeling lost and toughing-out your troubles alone. L. Ron Hubbard developed a unique process to help you through it.

Scientology Auditing *is* confidential. Mr. Hubbard intended it that way. The information is protected under Church policy and is recognized as confidential by many Government organizations.

"Traditionally, all communications between a minister and parishioner have been privileged and confidential. That is certainly the case in the Scientology religion, and this trust is never violated. In fact, the Church would invoke all legal protections under its clergy-penitent privilege to safeguard this confidentiality.

The Auditor's Code requires a minister to never use the secrets divulged by a parishioner in an auditing session. The information given in trust during an auditing session by a parishioner to a minister is considered sacrosanct by the Church and Church ministers. All such information is

kept strictly confidential by a Scientology minister and the Church."
- Church of Scientology International

The Church of Scientology doesn't share parishioner information with any government entity. Government issues are dealt with through personal contact with the individual member and the Government officials. Churches of Scientology all follow the same strict Auditor's Code. The Auditor's Code is referenced in the back of this book.

This Code, in Scientology, is professional and strictly followed. It's followed by *every* Auditor. When it's violated, the Auditor is required to see the Qualifications Officer. This is where the Auditor will be shown the policy on the violation, how to correct it, what the Auditor should restudy and then retrain on that area until their skills are perfect. Auditors normally get through the Study Program in a day to a week. Rarely does it take longer.

If this Auditor committed a violation in Confidentiality. This Auditor would go through the Ethics system in the Church. The exact procedure taken would be up to the information in Church policy, references and the *Introduction to Scientology Ethics*. Breakage in Confidentiality isn't treated lightly in Scientology or any other religion.

CHAPTER 24:
CONFESSIONALS OR
A "SECURITY CHECK"

L eah has mentioned that she has received a lot of Confessionals. She has even interviewed people who have claimed the same. But, what exactly are Confessionals?

Confessionals have been used throughout all religions. You may be familiar with the Catholic version of "Forgive me Father for I have sinned." Scientology isn't any different.

"Another part of Scientology's ethics system is a type of auditing known as a Confessional. Man has long postulated a means by which he could put himself on the right path. As long ago as 500 B.C., religions recognized that confession frees a person spiritually from the burden of sin. In Scientology, it has been found that a Confessional assists the person who has transgressed against their own and their group's moral code to unburden themselves and again feel good about themselves and be a contributing member of the group."
- Church of Scientology International

While Scientology Auditing is confidential, a Confessional is not the same action and is made available to those in the Ethics section of the Church.

The information provided to the Ethics section isn't to be displayed to Scientologists or general Staff of the Church. This data is only provided to the Ethics personnel to help the person address the things or patterns of behavior the person is doing that harms themselves and others.

These individuals sit down with you after having finished your Confessional. These personnel are trained in the actions of helping you take responsibility for the wrongdoings of your past. This will only make you feel happier, more able and capable of living your life without those wrongdoings on your mind. This does not lead to punishment. It leads to a learning program for you to better educate yourself and find a better way to handle things. If you've done damage, then it makes sense to 'make amends' as part of your learning to make up for things that hurt others.

You'll find the basic theory of Mr. Hubbard is to ensure the individual that committed the wrongdoing has an opportunity to help the area he once harmed. I have received several Confessionals. Why? They were either requested or they were my next step on the Bridge to make sure I take a look at how I'm choosing to handle things and not doing things that ultimately hurt me in the long run.

A simple example would be taking street drugs. You wouldn't punish someone for taking harmful drugs, but you can see that long term they are in lower physical condition, their mood changes at work and at home, and their overall productivity decreases. Many will fight for their 'rights' to do drugs, but when really educate yourself in the area, a life without drugs is so much more fulfilling and it makes it easier to achieve the goals YOU set for yourself.

In addition, a Confessional is very relieving. They're so precise. The process is painless. The Catholic religion definitely understood the importance of the confessional. Mr. Hubbard expanded on the concept so that people actually learned and benefited long term from the action, and didn't just feel better for a while until they did something else later they needed to confess.

Sane people want to do Confessionals to get their past cleaned up. That is why I love doing Confessionals.

"No man who is not himself honest can be free—he is his own trap. When his own deeds cannot be disclosed then he is a prisoner; he must withhold himself from his fellows and is a slave to his own conscience."
- L. Ron Hubbard

Mr. Hubbard isn't stating that everything you've ever done needs to be told to the general public. That isn't the point.

When you're able to tell the Auditor your wrongdoings, you're able to put those aside and focus on the future. Mr. Hubbard developed the Scientology Confessional for that reason.

Leah hasn't done a lot of these. If she did, you wouldn't see her going around spewing falsities. Her attention is stuck in the past and can't see the future, let alone what's actually happening in front of her today. Plus, when you hear about her getting angry and flipping out, it's because someone has learned or is getting too close to the unethical things she's done and she can't handle getting found out.

Confessionals aren't there to silence you. They are there as a relief process. They're meant to put everything out on the table and handle it. Responsibility goes both ways.

When a Confessional is finished, the Case Supervisor looks it over to ensure that the individual is happy, relieved and other specific indications. After the Case Supervisor it is sent to the Ethics Officer. This is where it is then consulted one-on-one with you.

Mr. Hubbard wrote specific references and policies for the Confessional procedure. These are followed without exception.

CHAPTER 25: THE "RANCHES"

This chapter revolves around Leah and Mike's statements on the Sea Organization and children. This includes their comments made about the beautiful properties that were hosting children for schooling, boarding and every other function of their lives.

Leah and Mike have decided to make the properties sound like something from a horror film. These properties were ranches in California. They were operated by Scientologists trusted in the supervision of children and trained in all things children. Oh, and these ranches were set up to help raise children of Sea Organization staff in the 1970's.

These children were staying here free of charge because their parents or their guardian was in the Sea Organization. This was in the past; this action doesn't happen in the present. It was a test project that definitely helped many but was later discontinued due to the amount of effort behind it.

Scientologists are only allowed to join the Sea Org when their affairs are in order and when their children are of legal age and are able to be successful on their own. This will allow for the mother or father to join the Sea Organization, on their own willingness and by their own decision.

Parents aren't "disconnected" from their families when they are in the Sea Organization. They're encouraged by the Church to visit their family, stay in touch and to update the Church on any requested days off to handle personal or familial affairs.

On the A&E show, Leah and Mike had paid some disgruntled former members of the Church to share their "experiences" at these properties. These stories were invented and were discredited at every turn by those who were there with the individual.

One individual sharing their "experience" even went as far as to state that she was "sexually abused". This was easily discredited by her best friend at the time. If this occurred at the time, she would've easily shared it with her best friend; she would've gotten the help to handle it. It wouldn't have been tolerated.

This is just another buzz statement used to drive controversy at the Church and to get their payout. The statements made were actually quite evil. They were uncalled for and bigoted at every turn.

"I grew up at the Cadet Org Ranch in Los Angeles, California. It's this beautiful area, it's right next to a reservoir, and it's surrounded by mountains.

"I guess I would say, like, if I were to describe my experience at the Ranch, it was something I would never give up."
- Saina, Former Friend

"We were able to go camping and we were able to go hiking. You know, obviously under reasonable supervision. But it was just amazing, the entire experience was like, you know, "Good now we're gonna do this." and we're like, yay!"
- Saina, Former Friend

"The boys would be skateboarding or playing football and the girls would be making up dances or reading in our

room or riding horses or going on hikes, but it was fun.

"We always were entertaining ourselves and we never were stuck to screens like this generation."
- Saina, Former Friend

"I have some of these fond memories of just cracking open a watermelon that we grew and just sitting on a railroad tie, just eating, eating the big ole watermelon.

"Or sometimes we would go and we would have our gardens, we would pick flowers. I remember we used to put the flowers into a vase and stick them in our rooms. It was fun that was cool.

"Or we would go swimming. We used to go swimming almost every day. And that was just for fun."
- Saina, Former Friend

"I grew up in the Cadet Org with Saina. I understand that there's a claim that she was sexually abused while she was the Cadet Org and the Ranch.

"I was there when Saina was there. Not once did Saina mention anything to me. But not only that, no one ever told me about any kind of sexual abuse that was happening. I never heard of any kind of sexual abuse.

"I'm pretty surprised, I'm shocked to hear about this happening because 20 years later she's talking these abuses that happened as though that happened – but realize 20 years have gone by. So then she's saying I was sexually abused. But in that 20 years, and even the time that I was there, I've talked to many people about our experiences there, I've talked to many people about different things that hove happened in those 20 years, with our friends and how we're doing now , and just different people who worked there, and never, ever did I hear about there being sexual abuse at the ranch."
- Saina, Former Friend

This information makes me want to get a law degree. I would love to fight these statements made by Mike, Leah and people like Saina in court. These would be dismissed in seconds.

Saina could've handled it (if it even happened) right away. She would have mentioned this to the supervisors and the Staff. It wouldn't have taken much but a simple communication and the incident would be corrected at once. It wouldn't be tolerated.

She decides to go on a TV show and tell a former actress and a conman a story about sexual abuse. Could it be the paycheck? The controversy? Saina's disgruntled mindset towards Scientology?

These statements aren't treated lightly anywhere. I stand with the Me Too movement. Vetting statements like these will keep it straight and effective.

I stand with respecting women. Men take them for granted. They aren't possessions, they're blessings.

CHAPTER 26: THE GREATEST GOOD

I have discovered what Leah Remini is really against. She is against help and reason, she loves chaos and lies. It didn't take long for me to find this simple fact out and therefore I thought I'd share it with all who might be interested in knowing the truth behind the Leah curtain.

Therefore, what you're about to read is some very eye-opening and actually pretty logical analysis of what is going on and what she is actively promoting attacks on and bigotry.

When Leah attacks Scientology, she is not only attacking their members and their families, friends, co-workers, and their other relations. She is not only destroying families all around because people think that their relatives or in-laws are insane and part of a secret community.

The supported humanitarian efforts of Scientology cover a broad range of aspects to improve people's lives. Therefore, she would then be assumed to be against 90% of what Scientology supports. Millions of hours and millions of dollars of generous donations pour in week after week and month after month toward these campaigns and programs that assist people in times of need, times of change, times of awareness, and times of hope.

She is against human rights awareness. She is against over two-hundred million people of all ages becoming aware of their 30 inalienable rights as a human being. This education actually prevents human rights violations and also protects those who are in third world countries that have no sense of human rights and thus are unaware that they are being violated every single hour of every single day. These programs are the tools that empower youth and adults.

The human rights initiative of the Church of Scientology is supported by two different parts, *Youth for Human Rights International* and *United for Human Rights*. These are two organizations for the same purpose of human rights awareness and two different public in order to make the message clearer to the audience.

This program is reaching people from all over the world. It is in over 150 nations and assisting people from all denominations, all backgrounds, all genders, and all races. It sees through all of the prejudice and all of the problems in society and does not judge and only uplifts and educates.

Leah is against these youth and these adults learning they have these rights and that they have them simply because they're human and not because they have to work for them or that they are only given to the chosen few. These are for everyone and everywhere.

The fact that officials are recognizing the effectiveness and help that the Scientologists are providing through their support of the Human Rights programs.

"I am proud to offer my encouragement and support to the members of the Youth for Human Rights International Leaders of Tomorrow Club. In teaching youth around the world the importance of human rights, you and your colleagues are creating valuable advocates for the promotion

of tolerance and peace…I commend your Club as well as the youth of the Church of Scientology for working to increase respect and dignity of all people in the furtherance of world tolerance and peace."
—Office of International Religious Freedom
United States Department of State

Or, the fact that over 500,000 students have been empowered with Human Rights education and over 12,000 schools worldwide have implemented the curriculum and its materials provided FREE through the Church of Scientology's support.

Also the fact that Governments and organizations are partnering with the Church's sponsored Human Rights initiatives to truly make human rights a reality to the tens of millions across 190 countries it has already made aware.

The recognitions and acknowledgments are never-ending:

What you have done to promote international human rights is second to none. There have been attempts by other people and other organizations to create and do some things on international human rights, but I think the Church's international human rights program has reached a pinnacle no one else has reached.
—Political Director, Labor Council, U.S.

Human rights is not an abstraction. It is a very real thing that happens every day, that we have to defend and advance and deliver. So the everyday situations presented in the PSAs are exactly the way to communicate human rights.
—Secretary, National Government, Philippines

I have seen your campaign for human rights. I myself have worked for human rights in different parts of the world for the last 20 years. I have seen no one else working to educate all people on their rights as you do.
—Politician, Sweden

And, she is also against the educators from around the world having a say in how Scientology helps and supports the education and awareness of their students...

I received the human rights material and have incorporated it into a fifth-grade lesson plan on human rights. I was most impressed with all the materials and would like to thank you very much. This material enhanced what we were teaching and brought to life the importance of human rights.
—Teacher, U.S.

The DVD of Youth for Human Rights is proving to be exceptionally useful to me. It is an extremely attractive and effective educational tool. I have used it on several occasions in my school. I have used it among approximately 180 of my classes as part of their training in Life Skills education. I am using it to educate my student volunteers from classes 8, 9, 10 and 12 for my Service Learning Project, in which girls have undertaken to educate about 150 slum children of the local community.
—Teacher, West Bengal, India

As a direct result of the course, supplemental videos and training materials, my students lead a community campaign on human rights education and have been able to help another nonprofit organization provide support for human rights of disabled persons. As a United States Peace Corps volunteer, I was not able to find a better program in the three years I taught in Azerbaijan. The program was used to teach more than 150 high school and college-age youth and to motivate them to be more active in human rights.
—Educator, Azerbaijan

Leah cannot continue to ignore the results of Scientology's Human Rights program. That has nothing to do with the other programs that they support. In fact, Human Rights are not something Leah has any clue about and she has no intention of letting others know about their Human Rights.

Mental Health Abuse

Leah is also against people having protection when they have been a victim of unethical conduct, illegal dealings, rape, drugging, and being held against their will and shocked with 480 volts of electricity – all from trusting a Psychiatrist.

Remini has been against these protections for a very long time. While in the religion she stated nothing about it, in fact, with all of the publicity she has had recently about nothing – she hasn't mentioned this at all as being something that she is distraught about.

The Church of Scientology co-founded and thus supports The Citizens Commission on Human Rights, or CCHR. They are a watchdog group in the field of mental health. Its mission is to eradicate psychiatric abuses and ensuring patient protections. That is what it does and since it was established in 1969 it has passed more than 160 laws protecting people everywhere and anywhere in regards to psychiatric abuses.

This organization operates from its headquarters in Los Angeles, CA where it operates more than 200 chapters across 34 nations. And, it has brought over 5,500 Psychiatrists to justice worldwide.

These are huge numbers but, let's hear it from the people Leah already hates:

"I join with Congress in recognizing the Citizens Commission on Human Rights for its longstanding commitment to advancing the fundamental freedoms set forth in the Universal Declaration of Human Rights and the Nuremberg Code. CCHR serves as a stellar example of the united power of individuals who achieve reform through dedicated efforts to better society and effective education and advocacy. We recognize CCHR for the many great reforms it has championed,

which today protect individuals against cruel, inhumane and degrading treatment and for its leadership role in raising public awareness so that dignity and human rights can be returned to all men."
—Member of U.S. Congress, California

"Honor those to whom honor is due. On their 40th anniversary, we broadly recognize CCHR's unprecedented fight in mankind's history against psychiatric abuses, it's protection of children from abusive practices and encourage CCHR's humanitarian work."
—House of Representatives, Mexico

"In recognition of your tireless, courageous work seeking to improve our society through your efforts in the area of human rights abuse, I extend my best wishes for your continued success and fulfillment."
—State Assembly Member, California

"CCHR has been instrumental in ensuring protection for the rights of parents and children in the field of mental health —above all in guaranteeing informed consent as the surest protection against a tendency to hasty diagnostic and inappropriate treatment."
—Member of the US Congress, Oklahoma

"CCHR is actually going in and protecting individuals, speaking to those individuals who have been damaged, helping them, making their story known."
—Clinical Psychologist, Denmark

"CCHR has been a steady force to broadly expose the drugging of children in Japan. They are a strong voice in protecting children in this country."
—Member of Parliament Japan

"The Citizens Commission on Human Rights has exposed the outrageous number of psychiatric involuntary commitments

in each region of France and has reported these to me. They have made me aware of the need for reform in this country."
–Member of Parliament France

"We want to commend the Citizens Commission on Human Rights for bringing the exhibition 'Destroyed Lives: Exposing Psychiatry' to our Institute. The exhibition was effective in enlightening both experienced staff and the next generation of staff."
—Executive Director, International Institute of Justice, Russia

On top of these voluntary successes, acknowledgments, and recognitions are the 700,000 people who are now informed about the abuses of Psychiatry due to their traveling exhibitions enlightening people worldwide.

Maybe Leah will think next time before she pushes the people who have been affected by Psychiatry into the corner and attacks the one effort that is making this kind of impact.

Drug Rehabilitation

All that Leah has said about Narconon is repeating the discrediting statements from "professional" doctors and experts who are paid off by the pharmaceutical companies and do not want people to come off of drugs.

Even her right-hand man, Rinder, had this to say about Narconon (5 years after he was expelled):

"I and you too, no doubt, have seen people's lives literally saved by Narconon. Narconon is worth saving not destroying."
- Mike Rinder

There is no way he was being paid to make the above statement, according to Mark "Marty" Rathbun (Remini and Rinder's former guru), he was being paid for three years to be Anti-Scientology thus far and making a "handsome living".

But, what about the tens of thousands who have been saved

from drug addiction or maybe the 16 million individuals now educated through their drug prevention educators going to schools, colleges, businesses, and everywhere else to deliver seminars to the masses in the name of drug prevention and rehabilitation.

These are the successes on implementing the Narconon Drug Rehabilitation Program across the globe. Of course, Leah *hates* these people:

As Chairman of the Senate Select Committee on Substance Abuse, I would like to take this opportunity to thank you and your organization for the work you have done in fighting substance abuse. Because of the hard-working Narconon program and other similar organizations, the current ideal of a drug-free society may one day become a reality.

The accomplishments of Narconon speak for themselves. The response letters from people who have participated in the program indicate total support for Narconon. Narconon's unique approach in helping addicts off drug dependence at a more rapid than normal rate is remarkable.

The fight against substance abuse must be a joint project involving both government and the private sector. I am proud to be associated with Narconon and encourage others to join the fight against substance abuse.
—State Senator, U.S.

The scourge of drugs remains one of the most difficult and vital challenges that our society has yet to overcome. This cycle of hopelessness must not continue, and only through the determined efforts of individuals and organizations such as yours can we prevail in this struggle. For the past 25 years, you have been actively involved in helping to prevent drug abuse, and counseling and educating those individuals who have fallen prey to the allure of illicit drugs. Since your founding in 1966, you have expanded to include Narconon Centers in

countries worldwide, strong evidence that your programs and methods have proven to be effective.
—Former Governor, State of California, U.S.

Narconon has a unique position in the rehabilitation field. It offers addicts a relatively painless drug-free withdrawal —something that most addicts and professionals consider impossible. It has developed effective programs at no cost to taxpayers, at a time when the [U.S.] government has invested billions of dollars in experimental approaches that have not offered satisfactory solutions.
—Medical Doctor, Drug Rehab Specialist, U.S.

I've now put nearly 4,000 individuals through the Hubbard detoxification program. I can say without a doubt that it works. It's still the only treatment that addresses the effects of accumulated toxins. And there's nothing else on the horizon.
—Medical Doctor, U.S.

I have acted as medical consultant to the Narconon program for 15 years. For the past decade I have studied the results obtained through the use of a detoxification method developed by L. Ron Hubbard, utilizing vitamins, sauna baths and exercise, which is a part of the Narconon program. Narconon clients, with histories of moderate to extremely heavy substance abuse, show a marked improvement in alertness, clarity of thought and general health by undergoing this treatment. Most also report a substantial reduction in their craving for drugs or alcohol. Published scientific studies of the technique have shown it to be successful in reducing the concentration of a variety of toxins and contaminants in body tissues, and I highly recommend its continuing use as an effective tool in the treatment of addictions.
—Medical Doctor, Canada

I will definitely apply what I've learned in future studies

and lectures at schools. No barrier will prohibit me from being successful anymore, thanks to Narconon's Learning Improvement Course. I'll advise all my other colleagues to attend this course. Keep up the good work!
—Police Inspector, South Africa

I write this letter based upon four years as a prosecutor in drugs for the Federal Department of Justice and 13 years on the Provincial Bench of this province. One of the very few functioning organizations successful in the rehabilitation of heroin addicts, in my opinion, is Narconon. Any support which this group can obtain from public funding is, in my opinion, very worthy.
—Provincial Court Judge, Canada

And, these are some of the successes of the Narconon program. I'm sure this is nothing like you've heard from the Fake News posse. They're all about what fills up their pockets.

But, of course, I would be crazy to list out all of the things that Remini is against. It would be a *very* long list of things. They are all very pro-survival activities but that is what threatens her and her agenda and she'd rather not let that happen.

But, as you can see, these organizations and programs are being implemented around the world and they are completely secular from the Church of Scientology. They are only supported financially and through their members, but they are solely their own entity and that is a fact backed up by the legal documents through the IRS and the US Supreme Court and the policies by the Founder of Scientology. These all will back that fact up.

It is the Scientologists' responsibility to do something about the world in which he lives in. The individual Scientologist has the solutions right in front of him and/or her. Either by donation or by physical action.

Therefore, the Church of Scientology has helped millions

through these secular programs that are so effective that they have changed lives for the better and improved communities where they were at their complete downfall.

You can see why Leah would hate all of these programs and organizations, they are helping people live better lives and she is not. She is doing the polar opposite.

Leah, if you finished reading this part, I understand how you could be upset. These are very in-depth and very correct chapters that you cannot ignore and they are actually under Freedom of Speech. Just like you, you can get away with lying and inventing stories. I can get away with spreading the truth as a journalistic figure on the subject of you because you are a "public figure".

CHAPTER 27: GOLDEN ERA PRODUCTIONS

T he Golden Era Productions complex has been the talk of apostates, especially Leah, F o r e v e r. This complex has had the most false information spread about it than any other property in Scientology. It is because it is gated off and isn't a public property which makes it easy for apostates to make up stories about.

Golden Era is a production studio for all Church technical films, music production, international events, translations, internet properties and even specific production projects for the religion. It's similar to other studios that are built in pleasant areas for creative focus and excellence. Skywalker Ranch is a good example of another production facility which is located north of San Francisco.

Golden Era is state-of-the-art in every aspect. It sits on 500 acres in Gilman Hot Springs, California. It has tennis courts, professional apartments, cafeterias, one of the largest sound stages in North America spanning 80,000 square feet and much more.

It's staffed by Scientology's religious order called the Sea Organization. These individuals work their tails off and are provided everything from lodging, food, transportation, library, medical, dry-cleaning, and more, all taken care of by the management of the Sea Organization.

The uniqueness of Golden Era Productions is simply that it isn't open to the general public. This is the same for other film production studios. Golden Era Productions can arrange for tours by reservation, clearance and a legitimate reason.

Leah Remini and Mike Rinder have stated some fallacies about Golden Era Productions that I'll clear up.

Golden Era Productions' Staff are taken care of. These individuals are hard-working, happy and content. You won't find another individual like a Sea Organization member.

David Miscavige, Leader of Scientology, looks after Golden Era Productions' staff very closely. He sees to it that they're looking out for themselves and for others. They can work hard, but they shouldn't ignore their basic necessities. They even have medical and dental care available on site.

Leah Remini and Mike Rinder aren't being correct when they make remarks about lack of basic necessities. This is also something others have falsely attacked Golden Era over the years, so there's nothing to it.

The transportation is simple. If a staff member wants to drive somewhere, they take a staff car that is maintained on the property by professional mechanics. They tend to go on group outings, couple outings and they sometimes even bike.

This is a distraction-free environment. It's also stress-free. The necessities of the Staff are taken care of; it is done this way so the Staff can focus on their duties without worry.

The ridiculous statement that was made recently by Leah Remini and Mike Rinder was mention of a "Hole". Speaking to Staff that has worked there, there wasn't a mention of a "Hole". There isn't even a pothole on the property.

The craziest thing is, this statement got the FBI fired up to do an investigation on Scientology in 2010. Where did it lead to?

The FBI found that there was *no* hole. One of the apostates actually stated this to the FBI. The following statement is what closed the case, even after their investigation:

"I have seen no violence on behalf of David Miscavige or anybody else at the upper levels of Scientology. I have seen no evidence of this thing they call the hole for the several years that I've been there."
- John Brousseau

It seems Leah Remini and Mike Rinder are running out of lies to spew. They used to be on the truthful side, it just didn't seem to go well with their insanity drive.

Golden Era Productions has even been slammed in the past by a "documentarian" Alex Gibney and an "author" Lawrence Wright. That is where it started to get slammed publicly.

There aren't ants on the wall, there aren't any holes and there aren't illegal dealings happening on the complex.

Are they jealous much?

David Miscavige does operate most of the Church projects from this very complex. Why? Because it's able to be a protective, distraction-free and inexpensive space for these special projects to take place.

Royal treatment for David Miscavige and other Church executives doesn't happen at Golden Era Productions or anywhere else in Scientology. They're only respected but, they aren't given anything more than a fellow Sea Org member.

I have met people who have worked at Golden Era Productions and they loved it. This wasn't something they were told to state, as Leah and Mike would say, they actually enjoyed it.

Leah's assistant, Valerie Haney, worked at Golden Era Productions for quite a few years. She didn't hold any executive position. She was a part-time event greeter, helped build the designs for sets and she was the fill in for extras in Scientology properties. Contrary to what Valerie has stated on A&E and anywhere Leah is blabbering, I'll share some statements she's made before she was bought and paid for.

During an interview done as the last step of the dismissal process, from Golden Era Productions (it was filmed):

"There was not one job that I had (in Scientology) that was not fabulous."
- Valerie Haney

Valerie sure was happy. She volunteered *many* statements about the Church, Golden Era Productions and the Staff that were positive. Didn't state any of it under duress, persuasion or convincing. Valerie would've had no reason to.

I know Valerie actually likes David Miscavige, despite what she is paid to say, this is what she's said about him:

"Mr. Miscavige was the most caring and considerate and awesome individual that you could work for."
- Valerie Haney

Mr. Miscavige actually assisted Valerie with a personal injury. Valerie wasn't a direct responsibility of Mr. Miscavige but when he found out that Valerie was injured, here's what he did, according to Valerie:

"I broke my leg and Mr. Miscavige found out about it. It was pretty amazing he dropped everything came down and saw me and wanted to make sure that I was taken care of. Made sure I went to the hospital, made sure I went to the best hospital. He wanted to make sure that I was getting the exact help that I needed."
- Valerie Haney

This happened on Golden Era Productions complex. It's a great complex, wonderful staff and great properties.

CHAPTER 28:
CLEARWATER

Leah Remini and her posse have said some pretty gnarly invented stories and statements regarding Clearwater, Florida and Scientology. The statements they have made are utterly false *and* easy to discredit.

This all really stems from the Church of Scientology owning a number of buildings in Clearwater to deliver to their international congregation. They have also helped purchase other empty buildings as part of a campaign to revitalize the Clearwater area. That is really all it is about. It is made into something "big" even though it really isn't "big".

No, Mike Rinder didn't actually try to visit his son like a normal person; this is what his son states:

> **"So during my cancer treatment, the whole cycle from beginning to end, he did not contact me once. He didn't offer to help pay the medical bills, he didn't maybe ensure that I was getting the best treatment that we could get. He did nothing. He was not involved at all. So I could have died. He wouldn't have even known.**

> **"I was in the sauna and two policemen come into the sauna, "We need to see you." So I got up, went out of the sauna.**

Basically said your dad is at the front of the building and he wants to see you, he's waiting for you. And for a moment you can think "Oh maybe there's a bit of compassion there" or care. But then you think "Well wait a sec, what's the only reason he would be standing in front of the Fort Harrison with a camera crew trying to come and get me, getting the police involved?" He is just trying to make himself right maybe or prove a point like "look how bad they treated us" and to create a fabricated story or something. And I said "I want nothing to do with him, I don't want to talk to him, I don't want to see him. I want nothing to do with him. I'm living my life and I'm figuring it out, and he can live his life and he's on his own with that. I want nothing to do with it." And they said, "Okay. So you want nothing to do with him?" "I want nothing to do with him."

"He doesn't care about me, he doesn't. If I had died five years ago, it would have just been like "Shoot—I need another angle now to cause trouble or whatever." I'm perfectly happy with him not knowing anything about me. I don't care. I don't live my life trying to prove something. Doesn't matter to me."
- Ben Rinder, Son of Mike Rinder

This was a case where Mike Rinder (Leah's co-host) tried to stage that the Church of Scientology wouldn't let him see his son. As you can see, Ben was open to talk to him but, when he found out that Mike was in front of the building with *cameras*, he declined the offer. This was the breaking point to even talking.

Clearwater is where Scientology's Founder established the area where the religious order could have a stable base on land. This would later be called "The Flag Land Base", named after the Flag Ship "Apollo". This was a landmark event and milestone in Scientology as *The Fort Harrison Hotel* was purchased and made into the official headquarters.

Yes, things have definitely changed and more expansion has occurred in Clearwater for the Church.

The Fort Harrison Hotel is now just a Scientology Religious Retreat and the Flag Land Base is the "Flag Building" that was opened after 30 years of planning, fundraising, and execution, in November 2013.

When operating the base for the *best* delivery of the counseling and training services of the religion to their international congregation, you're going to need facilities to facilitate the numbers of parishioners and tourists coming to Flag for these services. In fact, they are going to need facilities for lodging, food, weekend activities, their files, maintenance equipment, buildings for their supported humanitarian efforts, and even a basic public information center for those traveling with a person who's interested in finding out more about Scientology.

Yes, the Church of Scientology is also into improving the environment around them so that everyone in Clearwater and the surrounding areas are doing well. They involve themselves in community meetings and also strategic planning meetings with local businesses and churches. Attending these meetings and committees helps the church get a better understanding on what is needed and wanted from the community to be able to do better and to facilitate delivering their services to the Scientologists visiting their businesses as well as the current and growing population of Clearwater and surrounding areas.

That is what Scientology really looks at when it involves itself in the community. It doesn't look at the possibility of "taking over Clearwater". The Church of Scientology would rather just deliver its services to its members and carry on with its aims as an international religion.

"A civilization without insanity, without criminals and without war, where the able can prosper and honest beings can have rights, and where Man is free to rise to greater heights, are the aims of Scientology."
- L. Ron Hubbard, Founder of Scientology

This is too big for Leah and her posse to actually grasp. It is way too big. In fact, Scientology actually has its members opening businesses and also supporting local businesses so that Clearwater is benefiting every single year from the amount of money is being brought to the community each year.

"The Way to Happiness is an outstanding program which easily relates to the students and what they encounter in their lives on a daily basis."
- April Jones, Founder and President Saving Our Students Foundation of Tampa Bay

"Representatives from Criminon have been providing life skills courses regarding decision making and how to live a happier life to young people at the Pinellas Regional Juvenile Detention Center in Clearwater, Florida. Their teams of volunteers serve a vital role in helping to support the mission of the Department as we continue to provide opportunities for the youth in our care to be successful."
- Joseph Seeber, Superintendent, Pinellas Regional Juvenile Detention Center

If Scientology were to move out of Clearwater, the businesses would go away, the community would have to pitch in 300X the money that they already are just to cover the difference of the Scientologists and also the visitors of the Scientology facilities. I didn't even count the fact that the facilities of the Church cost a certain amount to maintain and that is paid to the City of Clearwater and therefore they wouldn't be getting this amount and their financials are dependent on the Church's funds coming in and their members coming for services.

Does Scientology really want to purchase all of the buildings in Clearwater? If nobody is going to take care of the building and it is going to go abandoned, why would someone who is fond of the community want that?

Well, the people who oppose Scientology for whatever reason or fear them "taking over Clearwater" will stop every possible way that Scientology will help Clearwater keep its buildings and artifacts and the pieces of history that make the city unique.

Trust me, if someone were keeping an eye on the buildings, Scientology wouldn't want to purchase the buildings that are historic artifacts in Clearwater, they would let the person who owns it and help that person out (only if he/she needs it).

In *The Way to Happiness* by L. Ron Hubbard, it is the precept *Safeguard and Improve Your Environment*. That is all that the Church of Scientology in Clearwater, Florida is doing. Leah and her posse are making it seem like World War 3 is happening and it isn't at the slightest.

The apostates are making it seem very chaotic but, in actual fact if you walk through Clearwater or Los Angeles and specifically near the churches of Scientology, you'll find nothing but peaceful religious services, happy members, and nothing going on but maintenance for their properties and attending community meetings occasionally or, when invited.

CHAPTER 29: CHURCH AND STATE

When someone is legitimately against what occurred in a corporation they handle it officially with that corporation. The hot coffee complaint of McDonald's was a true testament to this statement.

Leah Remini *knows* that Scientology wasn't to blame for anything that she did. Leah *knows* that creating the illusion that it is will only bring in more money and attention. This is the purpose.

We're dealing with a woman that cannot find an honest job. We're dealing with a woman that factually cannot handle upsets without blasting it in public.

Leah did not like being expelled from the Church of Scientology. Leah disliked that the Church of Scientology and Scientologists didn't actually care when she departed the religion. They didn't care at all since many opportunities were offered for her to become a winning parishioner like so many others.

Leah builds herself up to be a warrior. Leah builds herself up to be this "powerful" figure that was once a Scientologist, but she wasn't. This is untrue. This is strictly a public relations statement.

Legally, Leah Remini knows what she's doing falls under *Freedom of Speech*. This is a human right of everyone and is part of the United States Constitution.

Scientology and Scientologists cannot sue Leah Remini for libel, defamation and for trademark violations. This hasn't been thought by Scientology, but I have thought of doing it. Leah is dishonest, unethical and despicable.

Leah has "inspired" lawsuits against the Church of Scientology. These lawsuits are only regurgitation of the last 40 years of rumors, invented stories, defamation attempts and tries at extortion.

Take the recent lawsuit Leah has used for a publicity stunt. This lawsuit is just another attempt at extortion. These are the same individuals behind it.

Mike Rinder profits from these lawsuits regardless, he was seen raking in thousands from previous lawsuits regardless if they were lost. He still profited from "counseling the witnesses", choosing the attorneys and providing the "juice" for the lawsuit.

Mark Rathbun has stated numerous times throughout his interviews on his YouTube channel, Mike Rinder is being paid either way. It provides "dirt" for his agenda, money for his accounts and attempts to damage the reputation of Scientology and Scientologists.

How does Mike do this? It is simple. He does this by convincing attorneys that he's there to counsel the witnesses and provide legitimate testimonies. The attorneys or lawyers that are appointed have already been briefed on the purpose and are tracking on how they are going to attempt to extort funds to pay back the legal fees.

Factually, the information that is provided in these cases has been tried. Look into the previous forty years of the Church of Scientology's lawsuits. You'll find Mike Rinder, Tony Ortega and their other counterparts working together. The dream is to extort money from the Church to attempt to bring it to its knees.

This is a user on Twitter in reference to a lawsuit Leah "inspired" against Scientology:

"I strongly hope that this lawsuit brings Scientology to its knees."

Or, if that wasn't raunchy enough, this one is something:
**"Leah told me it was a cult.
I wish you all the best."**

Why would someone state this? This is wishing that a religion will be discriminated against. This is wishing the lawsuit is passed through without being checked for legitimacy.

Creating this hostile environment is a dishonest job. This is dangerous to Scientologists. This is what lies create a hostile environment.

I have spoken to people who heard about the publicity stunts of Leah (these are not Scientologists):

"From what I know Leah is one of the new haters of Scientology. She has made it her mission in life or something, she must really have done something wrong."

This person asked me a question on Instagram about a photo and we spoke over direct messages for a while about Scientology.

Want to know how her hate has hurt a children's view on religion? Here is what one child stated:

"Why in the world would I believe in a religion? It is stupid. God isn't real. I know more than anyone because I watched a lady named Leah".

This is a child. A child who doesn't want to grow up and follow a spiritual path. It's sad. This is all because of Leah Remini's hate on one religion.

I started asking around to random people, Scientologists and those who aren't Scientologists. I was curious how one individual could create so much hate. I was curious how so many people would support this effort. I was convinced it was a corrupt agenda.

I read into files of the lawsuits that were posed against Scientology in the last ten years. Each one had the same spin. Each lawsuit had the same statement, it was phrased differently. The lawsuits were started by the same lawyers, or they were new ones.

Leah Remini hasn't done this much research. This is new information to her. Research is important when consulting people about extorting money from an organization.

"I found that these lawsuits are dishonest, contradicting and frankly designed to defame Scientology's executives and services."

CHAPTER 30: THE INFILTRATION OF THE PAST

Some years ago, the part of the Church put in charge of protecting it, was actually infiltrated and went corrupt. This was the Guardian's Office and it almost crippled the Church and was finally disbanded after a difficult struggle. The idea of the Guardian's Office was Mr. Hubbard's, but due to infiltration the G.O. turned into something horrific.

Do you know who stepped up to stop this fearful entity? Mr. Miscavige found that the Guardian's Office had gone rouge. He decided to take action as a Scientologist, a Sea Organization member and because he knew it must be done.

"I, Michael Rinder, hereby declare and state: He (David Miscavige) overthrew what was at the time the most feared and powerful group in Scientology (that they were feared is exactly why they had gone so far in contravention of Church policy as they were only answerable to themselves)."
- Mike Rinder, Under Penalty of Perjury

What happened in the Guardian's Office after it was infiltrated was horrific. Some Scientologists were being beaten, pestered, blackmailed, threatened, dismissed, expelled, declared suppressive for questioning their authority, and more. The people trying to take over the Church were ruthless and helped create the stories that are spread around today. Their purpose? To take control and turn the Church into a cash cow of taking donations with no intention of delivering anything of value in return.

I'm not defending what happened to people when the Guardian's Office went rouge. That is why L. Ron Hubbard ordered the eradication of it. The Guardian's Office was the complete opposite of the true postulation of Scientology.

David Miscavige made it his responsibility to handle the eradication of the Guardian's Office. Mr. Miscavige went through administrative, personnel and even disaffected Scientologists to sort things out.

"I, Michael Rinder, hereby declare and state: He (David Miscavige) did not seek a high-profile position or attempt to 'take over' the Church. He was happy to have those who were charged with running the Church continue to do so and have no part of it."
- Mike Rinder, Under Penalty of Perjury

Mr. Miscavige destroyed it by exposing crimes, aiding the ethics and justice procedures of these individuals, reporting incidents to law enforcement, contacting L. Ron Hubbard for further instruction on uncertain situations and handling the judicial matters they had caused.

"I, Michael Rinder, hereby declare and state: The overthrow of the Guardian's Office began what I have seen to be a virtually unending history of personal attacks against him (David Miscavige). He didn't change, he merely became a known name and high-profile target."
- Mike Rinder, Under Penalty of Perjury

Leah Remini has trumped-up data. She's stating that Scientology is this way nowadays. It isn't. She's just trying to scare people with this rogue effort from decades ago.

Scientology transformed for the better afterwards. L. Ron Hubbard wrote advanced policies, references and procedures to control things before they get anywhere near such levels of corruptness.

It's utterly unjust that Mr. Miscavige would go through all of this to rectify the misconduct and then to be picked apart for doing so. I presume this is how Leah and Mike's mental process works.

I couldn't associate with a man that states one thing under penalty of perjury and then permits the polar opposite to be declared. Mike was part of the proceedings, he was part of the ordeal and he has stated things off-record about it, too.

He does confirm Mr. Miscavige's courage and bravery under oath. He has validated Mr. Miscavige many times and even though it is not obligatory, it is definitely gratifying.

"I, Michael Rinder, hereby declare and state: It would shock most people that anyone (David Miscavige) would work so hard for so little material reward. It certainly gave pause to ABC News when they saw it with their own eyes."
- Mike Rinder, Under Penalty of Perjury

Mr. Miscavige *does* care about his fellow Sea Organization members, Staff Members and the Scientologists. Mr. Miscavige demonstrated this by eradicating the Guardian's Office despite criticism, threats, extortion, and media slamming – all for taking responsibility for something that wasn't his doing.

Mr. Miscavige is definitely not in need of any extolment or high recognition. It would be appreciated if those who attack Scientology take issue with Scientology and those who are in Scientology to fully understand all that he has done to stop the incorrect situations from happening in Scientology.

One man, Ford Greene, is from the Guardian's Office. He is one of the people that made it go rogue. He is expelled.

Leah invited Ford onto her TV program. This man has done more evil to people and to Scientology than Mike Rinder.

He claims that he has won more cases against Scientology. Why? He is trying to fend off attention on him and his affiliation with the Guardian's Office. Leah endorses his statement and forwards it.

Greene hasn't been in Scientology in over twenty years. He will never be in Scientology ever again. That is a fact. The claims that he has made against Scientology have been all of the things he has done.

> **"Leah says that he (Ford Greene) has won
> over twenty cases against Scientology."**
> - Mark Rathbun

There haven't been many cases that have been won against Scientology, and Leah never cites any cases specifically. Apostates have been filing court cases against Scientology to try to extort money for years. It is nothing new and they have no possibility of winning. Those cases which receive an initial victory are always overturned by appeal, and after the Church fully documents the truth needed for the re-match.

> **"First of all, the grand cumulative total of all cases won
> against Scientology, since its inception sixty years ago,
> doesn't even reach anywhere near twenty. And most of the
> 'wins' were before this guy was even born."**
> - Mark Rathbun

Greene is a deceiver. Leah is endorsing a downright fake. Why? It brings in money and attention. Investigations do not include criminals, prostitutes, con-men and bitter failures. Investigations deal with accurate and vetted details.

The Church of Scientology has been entirely different since the Guardian's Office eradication in the 80's. Mr. Miscavige has only ensured the policies and procedures are applied to continue to forbid it from happening again.

Mr. Hubbard left detailed programs, procedures and policies to scoping out and effectively ridding a Church of any future infiltrators. Yes, this does include the law enforcement and judicial procedures. These procedures are effective immediately after any concern is discovered.

Mr. Miscavige has pushed the religion through attacks, extortion, mistreatment and other experiences. Scientology has continued to flourish and spread its content. Scientology has merely stood its ground.

Leah Remini and Mike Rinder proceed to assault. The religion is continually flourishing and prospering despite the attacks. This demonstrates that the arguments are insincere and are brushed aside as annoyance and blatant discrimination.

Reality displays Scientology isn't involved in illegitimate activity or anything questionable. Those who claim Scientology is hasn't actually visited a Church of Scientology since the earlier days of the Guardian's Office.

I guarantee you; it isn't like those early times. The policies aren't revised to fit the infiltrator's plan. The policies of the infiltrators were annihilated.

CHAPTER 31:
CENSORSHIP

What will probably occur after this book has been out for more than a day, it'll be attacked ruthlessly by those who are against Scientology, Scientologists and any form of help.

This is the "behind the curtain" exposé on these attackers. It isn't based on conspiracy theories. This is what Leah leads them to do.

The first book I published through Amazon was technically a "booklet", it was below 100 pages. *The Truth about Apostates: The Scientology Story* and it wasn't produced with the help of the Church of Scientology.

When the property was published, I received coordinated attacks from Leah and Mike's followers. This included death threats, harassment, coordinated one-star reviews, blog posts and articles. It was a surprise that this property brought so much attention. It was just a little booklet guys, why so much effort to silence it and make it look bad?

The upside is their attention helped to bring more interest and more sales, so part of me is okay with the hate, because either way, the book sells. I've even had to re-issue it with more content and bonus material.

Escaping Leah is one of my more recent projects. These properties are thorough and they're produced in such a short time due to the need for the information that's lacking on the subject.

Leah Remini won't be happy with this property. I know many people who weren't happy with her botched property.

What happens when someone educated in Scientology speaks out? What happens when someone educated in religions speaks out? The apostates get hammered.
I speak to those who are sane enough to duplicate it. Duplication is key. People who cannot duplicate are worthless to themselves and to the people around them.

Censoring someone based on your ignorance is a really crappy move. Don't fall for the movement of ignorance. Stand up for yourself and for those around you. Get educated.

Leah was never a prominent member of the Church of Scientology. She was barely even a member. Don't let her convince you that she was ever a member, she wasn't. She had no interest is really making any Bridge progress and she's hardly a 'hero'.

The truth is always hard for those who are brainwashed to duplicate. No matter what people state regarding me, my religion, my business and my properties, I'll continue to push through. I guarantee you, I can be your worst nightmare. How? I'll ensure that you get the truth about a subject, regardless of what it is, through any barrier and any statement made my direction.

Publicity is the key to writing books, interviews and other factors. You'll have those who want to censor you because you're stating what you are and that is completely understandable. There will be people who disagree with my views and there will be those that want to stop me. I'll just keep on doing what I'm doing.

Leah and Mike will keep going as long as they're paid. That is the corrupt view. If it were really true, they would do what I do and completely disinterest themselves with the money flow and focus on the truth flow. You can earn money with the truth as well. Fortunately, the human body doesn't live forever, and dedicating yourself to false activities usually makes a person ill rather than healthy. They will pass away along with their hate and their posse who are relicts from a forgotten time.

That is the difference between truths and lies. Truth always wins in the end. Lies have a short life span. If you'd like to join the group of sane and responsible people, study the subject from *actual* members.

I'm getting tired of hearing people say "I know all about Scientology", "I don't need more information, I have all that I need" and "Scientology believes in_____".

The only reason why I would be tired of it is because I've studied Scientology. I do know a lot about it. I won't tell you all about it because that is a lot to state. I'll refer you to where it's already stated, by the Founder. Scientology means the study of truth, or the study of life.

Censorship can't be from the truth, it can only be from the lies. No organization wants lies spread about them. That would just cause a lot of confusion.

CHAPTER 32: THE END OF THE HATE SHOW

T he A&E Network production with Leah Remini and Mike Rinder finally came to a close. There are certain factors that were involved in making this happen.

Scientology has been consistently discrediting the show's topics, information, even down to their interviewees. Why? They're baseless attacks on Scientology. If they were the truth, the entity receiving the attack would take the necessary responsibility.

Leah and Mike planned out these episodes, they used soundbite techniques, they scripted the interviews and the whole layout of the show, and they paid the interviewees and even paid themselves. This was an investment through their investors and their posse.

A&E Network didn't have a plan laid out; they were going to run the program. This program was being "backed" by A&E executives: Robert Sharenow, Aaron Saidman, Eli Holzman, Elaine Bryant and Paul Buccieri.

The executives have received numerous communications from the Church of Scientology, Scientologists and their individual attorneys. There hasn't been any response back from A&E Network that was complicit of the religion being attacked.

It was obvious that A&E wasn't focused on "exposing" anything; it was providing a platform for attacking and specifically hating on Scientology. That's the truth. They were never going to stop it.

The Church of Scientology took to the general public to educate them, inform them and arm them with the information to promote religious freedom in their communities. This also meant that those of faith were informed about A&E and their discriminatory program, which overall caused complete uproar from the faith community directed towards A&E.

I wrote a book about their agenda called *The Truth about Apostates: The Scientology Story* which made many see Leah and Mike for themselves. A&E wasn't seen as a "family friendly" and "exposing" network as they were promoting through their PR Department.

No, this isn't some "tactic" in Scientology. This is ultimately just standing up for religious freedom and in the face of discrimination. This isn't any different than how people are standing up against human trafficking, drug dealing, sexual abuse and gun violence.

During this A&E show, Scientology received over 600 documented threats, acts of vandalism, violent acts, harassment and even a murder. No such show has caused so much violence to occur than Leah and Mike's A&E hate piece targeting their former religion.

Paul Buccieri was notified about this and did nothing about it. There were crowds of people outside of the A&E headquarters in NYC, nobody in A&E cared. There were bishops, reverends, priests, bishops, ministers and fathers that represented themselves in A&E headquarters requesting to meet with Paul, they were declined.

This wasn't just a case of targeting Scientology; this was a case against all religions. Mr. Buccieri declined requests from every religion. He was hiding in his office and ignoring all requests. That's very unprofessional.

Many have fallen for the trap of watching this hate piece. Many have believed it. Large percentages of these viewers walk into the Churches of Scientology to find out more. Some just ignore visiting a Church and continue to "know" about Scientology.

Leah and Mike have created uninformed public. These people are going to end up hating all religious organizations because of what they think Scientology is. This has been seen by the alarming number of threats and other forms of violence.

Don't think for a second that your religion is safe from Leah and Mike's money grip. It's sadly not. They'll find an even more despicable "special" and a platform that'll fall for their trap as well.

Let me just say, I'd hate to be the next platform that takes these individuals on. Leah and Mike got off scratch-free this time – I'm wising up for the next round. I've got properties lined-up and connections that are ready to fire off.

For now, it's the end of a hate piece against religions. It's the end of a witch-hunt against Scientology on A&E. Hopefully; A&E learned a lesson and doesn't discriminate against religion again.

CHAPTER 33: DANNY MASTERSON

This chapter is specifically regarding Danny Masterson and the allegations that were stated about him and other women. Unfortunately Leah has decided to heavily promote this situation in an attempt to destroy Danny, merely because he's a Scientolgist.

Danny grew up in Scientology. He grew up on the basic belief that all people are worthy of respect, understanding and love. Danny is still a Scientologist and still believes in all of this information.

There was an upset with a former girlfriend that did not stay a personal matter, so Leah and Mike decided to coordinate an attack on Danny. Since their "high roller" (Paul Haggis) received allegations against him about domestic violence charges, these guys had to project onto Scientology what they're guilty of themselves.

Yes, this would mean that Leah and Mike coordinated victims, testimonies and a court case against Danny. It was all planned to occur right after the official notice of the cancellation of their A&E Network's program bashing Scientology.

This was all planned to get the attention off of their cancellation and onto a man who has only had help on his mind. This was an attack that cost a man his career and all for their public relations fix.

When Leah Remini and Mike Rinder fail, they throw a fit. This can be seen through their blogs, websites, interviews and any other platform that they've got their hands on.

These allegations are from people Danny Masterson had intercourse with consensually and then later stated it wasn't consensual. This, in this society, is deemed acceptable, even if it costs a person their career.

Obviously Leah and Mike are in need of some reality checks. Obviously I'm aware that they're in need of some and it's apparent that they're not aware.

I'm seriously against sexual abuse. I've had close friends and people I've associated with speak up. I'm aware that this is frowned upon and I'm aware that it's hard for those to speak up and stand up.

There's no doubt in my mind they had intercourse, especially his ex-girlfriend. It's bound to happen. Claiming that Danny raped them is absurd. This is completely against his integrity and he follows it very well.

I'm sure that Danny will work out how to appeal this lawsuit. The Church hasn't a part of this except for that it's his religion. Scientology doesn't tolerate abuse of any kind and frowns on those who are truly rapists and abusers. The attention shouldn't go on Danny. The attention should go towards the original person, Paul Haggis. Paul is the overall reason Leah and Mike have decided to back the allegations made against Danny with money and publicity.

It's a tough game with Leah and Mike. I've finally detailed every single slimy trick. Ultimately the justice system will look at the facts and make the correct judgment. Leah loses again.

I know the future plans. I know the future sources of the allegations will come from. I know a lot of things about Leah, Mike and their posse.

It'll be interesting to see how they like the truth. Truth wins and lies die.

Goodbye for now.

DOCUMENTS

This is the affidavit of Mr. Hubbard regarding "Fair Game" in Scientology.

I, L. Ron Hubbard, being duly sworn, depose and say that:

1. I am the founder of the Religion of the Church of Scientology.

2. From time to time, over the past 20 years I have written doctrine known as "Policy Letters" which are currently in use as administered by the Churches' ministerial staff.

3. On and around March 17, 1965; March 7, 1965 and December 23, 1965; I had cause to write three "Policy letters" entitled "Suppressive Acts Suppression of Scientology and Scientologists The Fair Game Law" (7 March 1965 and 23 December 1965) and "Fair Game Law Organization Suppressive Acts The Source of the Fair Game Law" (17 March 1965).

4. These policies were written with the intent to remove some of the fundamental barriers from the progress of the Church and its parishioners.

5. The intent, as written by me, was simply to make it clear to all Scientologists that those who actively attempted to block our forward progress could no longer be considered a member of the group and thusly not be afforded the protection of Scientology Ethics as so covered in the volumes of policy on the subject of ethics as written by myself.

Scientologists in good standing are protected by the ethical policies of the Church against suits or disturbances of any kind by another Scientologist. Recourse from any such action is immediately available to any Scientologist via a Chaplain's court which is held by a Scientology minister. His function is to settle all differences amicably.

6. There was never any attempt or intent on my part by the writing of these

policies (or any others for that fact), to authorize illegal or harassment type acts against anyone.

7. As soon as it became apparent to me that the concept of "Fair Game" as described above was being misinterpreted by the uninformed, to mean the granting of a license to Scientologists for acts in violation of the law and/or other standards of decency, these policies were canceled.

The handling of a Suppressive person with regards to the fact that he is not accepted within the Church and may not avail himself of Chaplain's Courts and other services of the Church due to the fact that he causes trouble and does not make personal gains, remains a stringent Church policy.

Signed this __22nd_ day of ___March__ 1976.

(signed)

L. Ron Hubbard

L. Ron Hubbard Policy Letter regarding "Fair Game"

HUBBARD COMMUNICATIONS OFFICE
Saint Hill Manor, East Grinstead, Sussex

HCO POLICY LETTER OF 21 OCTOBER 1968

Remimeo

CANCELLATION OF FAIR GAME

The practice of declaring people FAIR GAME will cease.
FAIR GAME may not appear on any Ethics Order. It causes bad
public relations.

This P/L does not cancel any policy on the treatment or
handling of an SP.

L. RON HUBBARD
Founder

LRH:ei:cden
Copyright (C) 1968
by L. Ron Hubbard
ALL RIGHTS RESERVED

This is the receipt of just ONE payment to Marc Headley for a rumor filled piece on Tom Cruise and Scientology. That figure is $10,000.00. The fact is Marc is part of the ASC and they're getting this income.

This is the IRS tax form for Marc Headley based on his income on attacking Scientology and its members through working the tabloids.

MH00002

Ryan Prescott

Mike Rinder's Handwritten Letter to David Miscavige

Mike Rinder
21 August 2003

Re: My Honesty

Dear Sir (David Miscavige),

Thank you for coming by to see me and _____ tonight - and I want to apologize for wasting your time and creating further enterbulation. I sat down and really did some soul searching with the assistance of the others as I obviously still had not confronted the depths of my out ethics and suppressive acts.

Many times I've looked at the overts I've committed when I have lied to you, and I've always had the idea that it was bad because it had caused upset - but not really confronted it as a basic violation of integrity, and therefore something far more fundamental and degraded - it is a reflection of my cowardice and lack of integrity that I would do this and it's just black and white wrong and a low-toned suppressive trait. I've done it many times with you and have always had some justification for it that I then didn't really confront it for what it is. I finally confronted this for real - there's no justification or Q&A about it. It's wrong, it's low-toned, and especially under the circumstances of being in the midst of a war, it's suppressive. I don't mean it's OK at any time, it's not - but the times I have done this with you have been when my "neck" has been so precious to me that I have been willing to put you and the Church in danger because of it.

I looked at a lot of things that finally opened this door - because I felt I was still to some degree trying to hold onto some rightness - which is why I didn't answer "me" when you asked who was the worst last night, and the comm lag tonight.

I went back to the time in CMO CW and the "successful actions" from that time. I've always hung onto the idea that there were things right about that time, and the operating basis with (illegible) was to always "be a good subordinate" and always say things are under control - unless it was reporting on someone else being a screw-up. But never was I a screw-up or responsible for anything wrong other than "handling someone else". This is the thing I confronted - that whole scene was an out-ethics sham. I see now this false assertion is just that - a false assertion that I've held in place to prove I'm right.

This then led (lead) me to really confront my integrity with respect to telling the truth and how I hate myself about this no matter how I justify it.

I know I have taken a long time to have this realization - and you have pointed it out to me many times and I've never been willing to look at this for the black and white issue it is - because it's a point of my own integrity first, and violating my own integrity has caused terrible results.

I do appreciate your insistence that I actually confront this - it actually was a major realization and relief to see something that is so obvious to you and others. With all the justifications I have had in place, telling the truth under certain circumstances was in my universe no different than telling a lie or withholding - but that is no longer the case, as I've finally recovered my integrity on this and will never operate in this suppressive fashion again.

This is OK,

ML (Much Love),
Mike (Rinder)

The handwritten document can be found on STANDLeague.org

Ryan Prescott

Mike Rinder's Affidavit explains all the false rumors being spread by apostates. This was written in 1994 amongst a former case against the Church.

UNITED STATES DISTRICT COURT

FOR THE CENTRAL DISTRICT OF CALIFORNIA

CASE NO. CV 91-6426 HLH(Tx)

CHURCH OF SCIENTOLOGY INTERNATIONAL a California Non-Profit Religious Organization, MICHAEL RINDER	DECLARATION OF

Plaintiff,

vs.

STEVEN FISHMAN AND UWE GEERTZ,

Defendants.

I, Michael Rinder, hereby declare and state:

1. I am a Director of the Church of Scientology International (CSI). I was raised in the Scientology religion and have been a staff member in the Church since 1973. As such, I have personal knowledge of the facts set forth in this declaration and if called as a witness, I could and would testify completely thereto.

2. As a Director of CSI, I have seen the filings made by the defendants and their lawyers in this case over the past six months.

3. Clearly, the focus of the defendants has not been on trying to disprove the defamation of which they were guilty or even to address issues related to the defamation. Instead, they have sought to turn this case into a

witch hunt of the Scientology religion. In doing so, the paid witnesses have specifically targeted the leader of the religion, David Miscavige, for their abusive lies and outrageous accusations.

4. Why would defendants and their counsel devote such an inordinate amount of attention to a non-party such as David Miscavige? Why would defendants' counsel's mercenary witness expose their lack of credibility so plainly by their resort to such outrageous and false allegations about him when he never had any involvement with Fishman, Geertz or this case? It is apparent that their effort to denigrate the leader of the religion is part of a campaign to create a false impression of, and thereby, denigrate Scientology. The lies that have been propagated in this case are vile beyond description. Their purpose, as made clear by Graham Berry himself, is to use them as a threat to extort funds from the Church. They have gotten away with this barrage of lies so far, and as a consequence, Berry now has the precedent of this case to use to create a future threat that he hopes will prompt CSI to pay to make him take his lies and go away.

5. David Miscavige prevented the Aznarans and Youngs from carrying out what would have been a catastrophic turn of events for the religion. Vicki Aznaran and Vaughn Young were involved in a scheme to pervert the scriptures of L. Ron Hubbard for their own profit. They were caught and stopped by David Miscavige. For this, every Scientologist is grateful. Even then, they were given the opportunity to redeem themselves within the Church. While they now rail against Mr. Miscavige and unleash the foulest lies about him their imaginations can concoct, any Scientologist would have thought it totally proper under the circumstances for those people to have been expelled from the Church without a chance for mercy. However, he gave them another chance. I know that he personally spent many hours with both Vicki Aznaran and Vaughn Young trying to help them regain their self-respect. They decided that rather than face those whom they had betrayed, that they would leave staff. Mr. Miscavige even helped Aznarans to get themselves established in a new job. They were encouraged to continue in Scientology and treated civilly, as even they have testified elsewhere. Yet, all this being true, the Youngs and Aznarans still have deep-seated hatred for Mr. Miscavige and have used this litigation to vent that hatred and to seek millions of dollars for their silence. There is no justifiable explanation for this, just as there is no explanation for savages dismembering missionaries who work for years helping them overcome poverty and disease. One can seek to help others and treat people with compassion and dignity, but the blind hatred harbored by a few cannot be restrained, no matter how hard one might try.

6. These people have gathered around them a few others who are bitter and harbor an unabiding resentment of Scientology and what it stands for and for their own failures in the Church. They view the Church as their "lottery ticket" and pursue their jackpot with lies and threats at the expense of the millions of happy and satisfied members who support the Church with their time and donations. The Aznarans and Youngs are joined in that pursuit by the likes of Hana Whitfield, Andre and Mary Tabayoyon, Larry Wollersheim, Steve Fishman, and Gerry Armstrong. Though they either do not know David Miscavige, or had some remote contact with him many years ago, they are willing to make vindictive allegations, not based on personal knowledge or the truth, and defame him personally and as the leader of the religion. The tactic is as transparent as it is unconscionable – spread venom in the hope that the victims of the hate campaign will eventually be forced to buy their silence so the Church can get on with its real purpose of expanding the Scientology religion and helping more people.

7. While these so-called experts have no personal knowledge concerning David Miscavige, I do. I have known and worked with him since 1976.

8. The sheer volume of despicable allegations made about him are intended to create the false impression that where there is smoke there is fire. These "witnesses" know only too well from their experience in the Church that the tactic of telling bigger and bolder lies has been a strategy employed against the Church in litigation for years. Tell enough lies, and make enough allegations, and impression will be created which accomplishes the end of destroying a reputation no matter how untrue the allegations are. Public figures are especially susceptible to this fraud as any study of history shows. Jesus Christ was crucified based on the false accusations of Judas Iscariot and the prejudice of the Romans.

9. Pontius Pilate listened to the lies about Jesus and the Christians. The Germans bought the lies about the Jews. Innocence does not prevent the lies from being told. And when those lies fall on ears opened by bigotry and deaf to the truth, irreparable harm is done. Defendants' tactics in this case are a study in this technique.

10. I know David Miscavige personally. As such I know him to be com-

pletely honest, and sincerely dedicated to helping people. For what he has done to expand our religion, he has the respect and admiration of millions of Scientologists. And for this same reason, he has earned the enmity and particular scorn of those with a vendetta against Scientology.

11. In the last decade, he has personally done more to ensure Scientology is standardly applied and made more widely known and available than any other single individual. After L. Ron Hubbard, the Founder of Scientology, passed away in 1986, the religion entered a new phase. While there will never be another L. Ron Hubbard, his death marked a time of potential disruption and upheaval, and Mr. Miscavige shouldered the responsibility for not only keeping the scriptures pure, but for guiding our religion into a time of great stability and rapid growth. He never sought personal power or aggrandizement; he was thrust into the position he currently holds precisely because he is so dedicated to helping others through our religion. It is because he has demonstrated time and time again his integrity and selfless willingness to serve for the good of others that he enjoys the support of the staff and parishioners of the Scientology religion.

12. I have spoken to him often, and spent a considerable amount of time working with him on various matters from the positions I have held throughout the years. I know from my own observation that he works sixteen hours a day, seven days a week without respite for only reason – his sincere dedication to bettering the lives of others. He and his wife live in a single motel-style room. He eats with the rest of the staff in the communal dining room, he drives his own car and carries his own bags. He regularly partakes in general group activities. It would shock most people that anyone would work so hard for so little material reward. It certainly gave pause to ABC News when they saw it with their own eyes.

13. Until 1981, David worked, like hundreds of other Church staff, in positions that dealt with the internal operations of the religion. Apart from the staff he dealt with directly as part of his duties, few knew who he was. I never heard an unkind word said about him. That changed when he took action to protect the future of the Church by taking over and disbanding the Guardian's Office. This story has been recounted before, but there are three things about it that bear repetition. First, what he did took an enormous amount of courage, for with no authority other than the moral authority of someone dedicated to the well-being of our Church, he overthrew what was at the time the most feared and powerful group in Scientology (that they were feared is exactly why they had gone so far in contravention of Church policy as

they were only answerable to themselves). Second, even after having achieved this feat, he did not seek a high profile position or attempt to "take over" the Church. He was happy to have those who were charged with running the Church continue to do so and have no part of it. Third, the overthrow of the Guardian's Office began what I have seen to be a virtually unending history of personal attacks against him. He didn't change, he merely became a known name and high-profile target.

14. Over the last thirteen years, I have seen a parade of personal attacks levelled (leveled) at Mr. Miscavige which would have caused a less determined and less capable individual to give up and relinquish the position of "lightning rod" for anyone seeking to disrupt or destroy the Church. The first years saw attacks by government agencies, since proven totally false and unfounded, and documented by the government's own files gained through the Freedom of Information Act. These attacks went on for more than a decade. Government agencies amassed a huge volumes of files on him personally, and were aided by civil litigants who also jumped on the bandwagon and targeted Mr. Miscavige with their spite and malevolence. And in the face of this, when it would have been so easy to give up and walk away, never to be vilified or attacked again, I have seen him persist, because what he was doing in Scientology is important and invaluable to all those who are helped by L. Ron Hubbard's technology. That determination was buttressed by the fact that none of the accusations made about him were true.

15. Mr. Miscavige is very approachable and friendly. He gives regular briefings to Scientology parishioners and staff in our Churches around the world. I estimate that he does such public briefings about 35 times a year. He stops and talks with the staff and public everywhere he goes. I have been with him on many occasions where he has stayed until the early morning hours to talk to individuals who remained after one of his briefings. It is remarkable how many people know him and approach him as a friend. Thousands write to him to request his assistance on a wide variety of topics, and he always takes the time to help or see that help is gotten.

16. It is David Miscavige who has been the driving force in getting every single book, and all materials of the Scientology Grade Chart, fully and strictly in accordance with the writings of L. Ron Hubbard. Every Scientologist is eternally thankful for this because it means the full availability of the complete Scientology scriptures as written or spoken by Mr. Hubbard. He took no credit for this accomplishment, though those of us who are aware of the enormous amount of time he spent working to make this goal a reality know

that the credit he so graciously gave to others, in fact, belonged to him.

17. Perhaps less important in his eyes than what he does internally in the Church, he has directly and personally given a new face to Scientology through his appearances in the media, responding eloquently and effectively to the same, discredited allegations that have been again dragged into this case.

18. And it is also David Miscavige who made the tax exemption by the IRS possible. It is he who personally walked into the front lobby of the IRS National Headquarters and through two years of persistent work, ultimately brought about a peace with the IRS that had seemed impossible. But perhaps the most telling point is this: it was the IRS targeting individual Scientologists, merely because they were Scientologists, that motivated him the most in this endeavor. Again, he didn't take credit for this, he has told me many times that he felt it was his duty to all Scientologists to carry this off so they would be free to practice their religion just like those of other faiths.

19. I have observed through the years David's dedication to helping his fellow staff in the Church. It is he who raised the standards and conditions for staff members by insisting on constantly upgraded living quarters, dining areas and other staff facilities. It is he who has insisted on staff enhancement programs, and recreational facilities being provided for the staff of the Church. Absurd allegations of slave labor being employed in the Church turn my stomach. I know the truth. They are lies, and those who utter them know them to be lies.

20. Mr. Miscavige has been the driving force in establishing the ideal school where my children have an environment free from drugs and crime. My children and their peers know him as a friend and think the world of him for his thoughtfulness and care for their well-being and their education.

21. I know his compassion from personal experience. While Vicki Aznaran makes cruel claims concerning the death of my infant daughter, she does not know what in fact occurred, or if she does, she is simply lying to try to create a false impression. In this time of great personal upset, David and his wife Shelly supported my wife and me beyond what could possibly be expected by anyone – seeing to our personal needs, arranging for the most highly

trained auditors to give us spiritual counselling (counseling), arranging plane fares and reservations, helping with the funeral arrangements and making it as easy as possible in every fashion imaginable for us to come through this upsetting time. I resent any implication that has been made to the contrary by Vicki Aznaran – her statements are beneath contempt.

22. On many occasions I have seen David go out of his way to help others. I well recall two times where I took ill and it was David who called the doctor and personally ensured that everything possible was done to help me recover. He contacted the doctor (both occasions were late at night and required tracking down doctors in the middle of the night) and ensured I was properly treated. It would have been easy for him to let someone else take care of me, but he did so personally, and would not leave or rest until the matter was resolved. These are things I will never forget.

23. I have seen him act in a similar fashion with many others. As I work with him often, and know many of the people that know him, I am aware of the high regard in which he is held by Scientologists and those he comes in contact with. I have never heard a negative statement made about him by anyone other than those who seek to extort money from the Church. It really is that simple.

24. Comparing what I know to what I read in the declarations of these paid "witnesses", makes the lies even more vivid and callous. There is no resemblance to the individual I know that can be drawn from the innuendo, allegations and falsehoods that are written about him. To believe the statements of this tiny handful of spiteful apostates, in the face of such overwhelming evidence to the contrary, would be to listen to the testimony of Judas Iscariot. Their lies are no less bold, baldfaced or malicious.

I declare under penalty of perjury under the laws of the United States of America that the foregoing is true and correct.

Executed this 11th day of April, 1994.

Signed,

Michael Rinder

This is an affidavit from Amy Scobee as part of the process of leaving staff at the Church of Scientology. She wrote this willingly, voluntarily and happily.

I, Amy Scobee, being duly sworn, do hereby state:

1. I am over 18 years of age and I have personal knowledge of the matters set forth in this affidavit. If I were called as a witness, I would be competent, willing and able to testify to what I state herein without reservation.

2. I am currently terminating my staff career with the Church of Scientology Flag Service Organization (*FSO*) and my membership in the Sea Organization (*Sea Org*), a religious commitment that binds the most highly dedicated members of the Scientology religion together, each of whom has pledged eternal service to the religion. Members of the Sea Org are wholly responsible to the Church of Scientology for which they work and are subject to the orders and directions of that church's Board of Directors. To symbolize their eternal commitment to the goals, purposes and principles of the Scientology religion, members of the Sea Org sign a covenant which extends this commitment for a billion years. Sea Org members are dedicated people, working without pause to carry out the mission of the Scientology religion.

3. I am terminating my membership and employment with FSO and I am doing so in the routine fashion according to Scientology policy and scripture. I am making this affidavit as part of this procedure and this document is to clearly communicate the whole picture. The statements in this affidavit are true and I am making them voluntarily and am doing this so that no one can make any claims to the contrary later.

4. In May of 1978, my mother introduced me to a staff member of Bellevue Mission of Scientology in Washington State. A Mission of Scientology is a beginning level Church of Scientology which offers introductory religious services. I found Scientology interesting and decided right away to find out more about it. I signed up for and took a course in communication at the Mission. From doing that course, I realized that I was a spiritual being, and I also learned communication skills. I have been in Scientology since I took that first course.

5. Around that same time I decided that I wanted to be a Church staff member and so I joined staff at the Bellevue Mission of Scientology. I held various functions and duties while I was on staff there. At first, I worked in the Public Division where I was responsible for introducing new people to

Dianetics and Scientology. I was also a Course Supervisor for various courses. The Course Supervisor is the person responsible for making sure that students that are studying Scientology courses rapidly progress through their courses and understand and are able to apply the materials they are studying. Also, at one point, I was the Course Administrator, which is the person who assists the Course Supervisor with administrative duties and ensures that students have the materials they need for the course they are on. I was on staff at the Bellevue Mission until late 1979.

6. All throughout my participation in Scientology religious services and religious studies, I was aware that I was doing so in a Church of Scientology. I never at any time had any misconceptions about the religious nature of Scientology. Throughout the time I have practiced my religion, I studied Scientology courses and received spiritual counseling ("auditing") from a trained "auditor". Auditing is a unique form of spiritual counseling comprised of a series of ascending levels of religious services that help guide a person to address traumatic areas of his past, and free him from their harmful effects. An "auditor" is a trained minister or minister-in-training who ministers auditing, the Scientology religion's main sacrament. Auditing has helped me to better understand myself and I also learned about the high ethical standards all Scientologists are expected to follow, these being a fundamental part of the Scientology religion. I have experienced spiritual gain and benefit from both the auditing and religious training I have done and I am fully satisfied with the results. I have an objective and subjective certainty that Scientology works when it is standardly applied.

7. I have participated in the advanced spiritual levels known as upper levels, or "OT Levels" or "Upper Levels", up through Level VII (there are levels up to Level VIII released to qualified parishioners). These Levels are confidential and are only released to parishioners who have achieved a certain level of spiritual enhancement and advancement. The materials that present these levels are kept secure and confidential and to review them, the individual needs to be invited to do so after satisfying certain general requirements. I know that there has never been any authorization to reveal, distribute or disseminate any of the OT level materials to the public, and I know that it is a sincere and deeply held religious belief that exposure to the information in the OT Levels before one has reached the appropriate level of spiritual training and development can cause spiritual harm. I know that the OT Level materials will never be released to the public generally.

8. In late 1979, I decided I wanted to become a Sea Org member. I left the staff of the Bellevue Mission and joined staff at the Church of Scientology of California ("CSC") in Los Angeles, California. I wanted to dedicate my life to achieving the aims that L. Ron Hubbard (the Founder of the Scientology Religion) set for mankind. I signed a symbolic contract dedicating myself to the Scientology religion for the next billion years, as do all Sea Org members. This

contract symbolized my devotion to the Scientology religion and I knew it to be a commitment for the rest of my life. In addition to dedicating their lives to the Scientology religion, Sea Org members are expected to uphold very high ethical standards and be extremely ethical in all aspects of their conduct. In this way, the Sea Org can continue to ensure that the Scientology religion is properly disseminated and practiced. I was aware of the fact that by becoming a Sea Org member and joining Church staff, I was pledging myself to live by such standards.

9. After a brief orientation as a new Sea Org member, I transferred to the Church in Europe, where I held a position over personnel for four months. In early 1980 I transferred back to the United States, to the branch of the Church of Scientology in Clearwater, Florida, known as the Flag Service Organization. I held several non-executive administrative positions there for the next three years. In July 1983, I transferred to the Church of Scientology International ("CSI"), in Los Angeles, California, where I remained until 2003. In 2003, I transferred again to FSO, where I have been up to the present.

10. I worked in an area of the Church responsible for recruiting interested Scientologists to become Sea Org members. I was staff of the Church in Copenhagen, Denmark at that time and was there until February 1980, when I transferred back to the Church in Clearwater, Florida. There, I held an executive assistant position until September 1980. I was formally removed from that position at the time because I engaged in an extra-marital affair contrary to the moral codes of Sea Org members. I was offered assistance and an opportunity to start on the Rehabilitation Project Force ("RPF"). The RPF is a voluntary program designed to assist Sea Org members who are having severe difficulties with their Church positions or who are not being ethical in their conduct. It is a program that enables a Sea Org member to participate in intensive religious study while he works on the premises for some time each day, doing things such as construction or gardening. This is designed to assist the Sea Org member to learn how to fully apply Scientology scriptures to himself and to others and to again become a contributing member of the Sea Org and the religion.

11. After eight months, in May 1981, it was determined that I did not need to complete the program and that I should resume my routine duties and functions as a staff member and I did so. I took up my duties in Clearwater and over the next few years until July 1983, I held various administrative positions in CSFSO, including two executive positions for brief periods. However, I again was found to be in severe violation of Church scriptures and still was being dishonest and again got myself involved in extra-marital   sexual misconduct. I was offered another chance to do the RPF, which I accepted. I transferred to the Church of Scientology International ("CSI") to do the RPF there.

12. In November 1985, though not finished with the RPF, I requested a review in accordance with Church policy and Scientology justice proceedings of my status as I felt that I should resume full duties as a routine staff member. This review found that I should resume my duties as a staff member and I did so in November 1985. Over the next three years, until September 1988, I held an executive function in CSI.

13. From September 1988 to January 1990, I was back on the RPF program that I had never finished, to resolve a spiritual matter that I needed to address. In January 1990, I graduated the RPF program and I again, in accordance with Church policy resumed my regular duties and functions as a routine staff member at CSI. From January 1990 until October 1991, I held several positions over the personnel area in CSI.

14. In October 1991, I was promoted to a senior executive position, on a committee. This committee is responsible for seeing that the various sectors which apply technology by Scientology founder, L. Ron Hubbard exist and are functioning. Over the next 11 years, until November 2002, I had a pattern of holding these senior executive positions for a few years and then, because of my neglect of my duties as an executive, I was demoted to a lesser position for a few months and then after I did well in the lower position, I was promoted back to a senior executive position again. My activities followed this pattern four times between October 1991 and November 2002.

15. While holding these senior positions, at times I abused my powers and responsibilities. In 1992 I used my position to obtain personal advantages and benefits over a period of nine months which resulted in thousands of dollars in unnecessary financial expenditures for the Church. In the early 1990's I used my senior position to protect a parishioner from being properly disciplined in accordance with standard policies of the Church, because I had a romantic interest in him. Once this person's true intentions and activities towards Scientology were discovered, he was excommunicated from the Church. I abused my power and violated policy by L. Ron Hubbard when I enforced harsh discipline on certain staff in 1993. This type of conduct is far below the standards expected of Church staff members, especially staff at the Mother Church in the positions I was in. In 1988, while on the RPF, I started a relationship with another man while both he and I were married to others.

16. In November 2002, I was formally removed from the last executive position that I held while at CSI. I held a lower post while my qualifications for CSI were reviewed. A few months later, in May 2003, it was determined that I was not qualified for CSI based on my poor performance record and because my moral and ethical standards were lower than what is required of a CSI staff member. However, I was again offered an opportunity to complete the RPF. I took this opportunity and was transferred to CSFSO to do the RPF and I am

currently on this program at present.

17. As described above, while I have had a number of difficulties during my staff tenure of keeping my ethical standards high enough to be a fully productive staff member, I have been on a number of important positions from which I have made contributions to Scientology that I am very proud of. I successfully applied L. Ron Hubbard's administrative technology to turn difficult situations into successful ones and to assist Churches of Scientology to expand and become excellent examples of what Scientology can do and offer to people. In my varied activities as a Sea Org member, I have been involved in many projects where I had to learn new trades and skills that I otherwise would never have known, but which I am now competent at and can even teach others to do. I have contributed as a staff member for the past 25 years towards achieving the aims of Scientology as given by L. Ron Hubbard -- a civilization without insanity, without criminals and without war, where the able can prosper and honest beings can have rights and where man is free to rise to greater heights. Because of what I have learned as a staff member, I know how to lead a group and move the whole scene of a group towards expansion.

18. I received assistance from other Sea Org members who are my friends and instead of being dismissed from staff due to the upsets I was causing, in May 2003 I was offered further assistance and another opportunity to do the RPF. As covered earlier, the RPF is a voluntary program designed to assist the Sea Org members who are having severe difficulties with their Church positions or who are not being ethical in their conduct. In May 2003, I was found unqualified for CSI and was thus transferred to the FSO in Clearwater, Florida, where I have been on this program. I have been working with another person while on this program, the idea being that I deliver auditing to him, and he delivers auditing to me on a turnabout basis.

19. While on the RPF, I have had numerous life-saving and life-changing gains from the auditing that I have received while on the EPF. I had become critical of other executives within CSI, but now I realize that this was because of my own dishonesties and harmful acts that I myself committed and then was withholding. Through the auditing I have received on the RPF, I have realized what underlies these impulses and have seen the cause of them, so that they are no longer able to dictate my actions. My whole viewpoint is 180 degrees different. I feel that I have recovered myself and have stopped "fighting imaginary enemies" because those people I was fighting, were truly my friends and were acting with sincerity in attempting to assist me in becoming a happier person. With what I have achieved in auditing on the RPF, I know that I can be productive and honest. While on the RPF, I have acquired the ability to help someone else and have learned how to audit another. I can confidently and I am more certain of my being able to produce the miracles from applying the scriptures than ever before. From my own auditing, I am aware of so much more truth. I have stripped away untold amounts of aber-

ration that I had "lived" with for a very long time. I no longer have held in place any "false disagreements" with people, but rather my entire outlook has changed.

20. However while on the RPF, I committed a severe violation of Church scriptures and engaged in an affair; in fact with the person whom I was supposedly helping to complete his RPF program. I was also this person's auditor, and my actions were a serious violation of the Auditor's Code, a sacred ethics code that governs the conduct of auditors. I realize that I have also contributed to endangering my friend's (the person I was working with while on the RPF) qualifications for staff in the Church and continued membership in the Sea Organization. I feel that over my history as a staff member, I have created too much harm for the Church and the people who work in it, for me to be able to fully make amends for these violations at this time. I have thus have stated my intentions to terminate my employment with the Church and end my vocation as a Sea Org member.

21. I am now going through procedures prescribed by Church policy to be able to leave in accordance with Church policy. As part of this procedure, I am going through a brief program to unburden myself of transgressions, so that when I start working after I leave Church staff, my life will be easier. I am not upset with FSO, any other Scientology Church or the Scientology religion. My attitude towards Scientology is that in the final analysis, it is the only thing that matters; and nothing will ever shake that belief for me. Everything that L. Ron Hubbard has written is truth and no matter what I do, I will contribute to making Dianetics and Scientology known so others can learn it too and lead happy and productive lives by finding that truth. Throughout my time as a Church staff member, I have had many personal gains from participating in Scientology training and auditing. I am now an excellent student whereas before Scientology, I could not understand what I was studying. I am so much more free and able because of the technology as discovered by the Founder, Mr. L. Ron Hubbard. I know that in Scientology I have the truth, and the technology along with it that is capable of setting man free. I am glad that I have had the opportunity to be a Sea Org member. I have gotten the ability to contribute everything I can toward one overall goal -- which is the universe returned back to its native state and impervious to the traps and faults of yesteryear. I had many gains just working on expansion projects and doing things that contributed to the overall purpose of the Sea Org.

22. In all my dealings with the Church and my Sea Org membership, I have observed that the Church has taken great care to abide by the law and has demanded the same from its staff. At all times, honesty, integrity and ethical conduct are emphasized as a hallmark of Sea Org members and when infractions, dishonesty or unethical conduct are found, the Church has taken appropriate action to get them rectified. There were times during my tenure as a staff member in CSI or FSO when I committed unethical acts, such as those

mentioned above. In other instances I neglected doing my duty when other staff trusted me to do so, and this created upset with the staff there as well. In each of these cases (many of these are well covered in earlier paragraphs of this affidavit), another Sea Org member has assisted me to become more ethical and has shown me that being honest with myself and others is a much better way to live life.

23. I acknowledge and agree that as a Sea Org member I have an obligation to maintain the confidentiality of information obtained in the course of carrying out my staff functions, including, but not limited to, non-public information, data or knowledge that I learned about the organization or staff of the FSO, Religious Technology Center, CSI, or any of CSI's affiliated Churches, Missions, or Organizations, such as their structures, security matters, finances, functions or activities, and information which has been orally imparted to me in the course of my having been a Sea Org member. By this affidavit, I acknowledge that the information I learned as a staff member was given to me in a relationship of trust and confidence. I acknowledge also I have a duty to FSO and CSI to keep the information confidential, whether or not I remain a staff member. I agree that my commitments to maintain such confidentiality fully in force whether I am a Sea Org member at any Church of Scientology or not, and I both acknowledge and reaffirm these commitments.

24. I have seen the Scientology religious film called "Orientation". I understand and believe that Scientology is a religion, and that all services that I received as a staff member of the FSO are religious, including auditing, co-auditing, confessionals, security checks, administrative training, technical training, cramming, and all forms of application of Scientology Ethics and Justice technology.

25. I have never been a corporate officer or director for any Church of Scientology corporation. I was a trustee of the International Hubbard Ecclesiastical League of Pastors "IHELP" from May 1995 until July 1996 when resigned. As a Trustee, I assisted in appointing directors for IHELP but I had no duties concerning the day to day functions of IHELP. Additionally, I was a trustee for the Association of Better Living and Education "ABLE" from October 1997 until August 25, 1998. ABLE is the organization which provides the social betterment technologies developed by Scientology Founder, Mr. L. Ron Hubbard. Again, as a Trustee, I assisted in appointing directors for ABLE but I had no duties concerning the day to day functions of ABLE. I have not been a corporate officer or director of CSI or FSO.

26. While a Church staff member at FSO and CSI, I have at all times been remunerated in accordance with Church policy, and I both agree and acknowledge that no Church organization or entity owes me any additional remuneration.

27. I am not under the influence of any drug, narcotic, alcohol or mind-influencing substance, condition or ailment such that my ability to fully understand the meaning of this Affidavit is adversely affected. I have not been threatened or coerced in any manner to make the statements contained in this affidavit, and I have made these statements of my own free will.

28. IN WITNESS WHEREOF I have set my hand and seal this 27 (hand-written) day of January, 2005.

_____
Signed by Amy Scobee

STATE OF FLORIDA)
) ss.
COUNTY OF PINELLAS)

The foregoing instrument was acknowledge before me this 27 (handwritten) day of January (handwritten) 2005, by Amy Scobee, who is personally known to me or has produced California DL B4924412 (handwritten) as identification and who did (did not) take an oath.

_____
Signed by Public Notary

NOTE: ALL PAGES WERE HAND INITIALED BY AMY SCOBEE DOCUMENTING THAT EACH PAGE IS TRUE.

THE PDF CAN BE FOUND AT WHOISAMYSCOBEE.COM.

Cost of an Anti-Cult Affidavit by Stephen Kent: $11,000

Professor Stephen Kent, a professor at the University of Alberta, has emerged in recent years, as a traveling crusader against academic scholars of new religious movements who threaten the profession's integrity by, inter alia, appearing as expert witnesses on behalf of religious movements.

Kent has recently appeared in Germany and Denmark to promote his crusade.

Anti-Scientologists have now posted on the Web his affidavit against the Church of Scientology in the well-known McPherson civil case. As far as I know, Kent has not objected to the posting, nor has he suggested that the document has not been faithfully reproduced. It is a document of 12,825 words (bibliography included). Of particular interest is the last paragraph:

"My curriculum vitae is attached to this report, and it lists all of my publications for the past ten years along with court cases in which I testified as an expert. For preparing this report I have been compensated at the rate of $200.00 per hour. I have worked approximately 55 hours on it. The exhibits that I plan to use in support of my opinion are included in my bibliography."

Thus, the cost of the affidavit comes to $11,000. Readers familiar with Kent's private and public production will easily recognize that most of the affidavit is derived from Kent's previous works. At any rate, if Kent really thinks that experts in "cult" cases should make $11,000 for each 13.000-words document based on their previous works they write, he may be right after all and "academic integrity" may, in fact, be in serious danger.

Massimo Introvigne, Feb. 18, 2000

Update on Stephen Kent's Expensive Affidavits: One Claims that Scientology Is a Religion, Cost of the Affidavit - $21,600
by Massimo Introvigne

I have commented before on Prof. Stephen Kent's crusade to preserve integrity in the study of new religious movements against monetary corruptions, and the (corresponding?) increasingly high costs of his affidavits. He has of course argued that scholars executing affidavits on behalf of new religious movements also receive significant amounts of money. Obviously, this is not the point. These scholars do not tour the world to lecture against money-induced corruption of scholarly studies about new religious movements. Kent does, and it is not unfair to suggest that he should be judged by his own standards.

For those who have heard Kent downplay the religious element in Scientology, a recommended reading is now Kent's affidavit in the Texas case EEOC v. I-20 Animal Medical Center, signed on November 9, 1999. In the case, EEOC charged that the use of Scientology-based training methods in the workplace violates Title VII since Scientology is a religion and not a purely secular training system. Supporting EEOC, Kent signed an affidavit to the effect that this is a case of "intrusion of religious concepts into the workplace" (p. 9). The courses contained "Scientology terms" that Kent now describes as being "purely religious".

In short, the courses "contained the Scientology religion" (pp. 12-13). Quite correctly, Kent concludes that Scientology is a religion based mostly on its notions of thetan and of past lives. We applaud Kent's reliance (at least) on mainline scholarship on Scientology in order to come to the conclusion that what others (including persons Kent should know better than any other) have described as mere "treatment" is in fact "a religious practice" (p. 18).

If somebody should accuse him of incoherence, Kent would of course answer that he always claimed that Scientology is also, but not exclusively a religion, a fine distinction probably lost to the audiences and courts that received Kent's previous wisdom. For the 19-pages affidavit, Kent "has been compensated at the rate of $ 200.00 per hour" and has "worked approximately 108 hours to date". That raises the cost of a Kent affidavit (although, admittedly, not a typical one) to $21,600.

ACKNOWLEDGMENTS

I owe my gratitude to those who have stuck by my side and understood my purpose loud and clear. To those who I've researched through.

I'd like to first give my admiration to my wonderful family. My family has done so much for Mankind through drug rehabilitation, criminal reform, character building and even through Church volunteerism. I've only been inspired by these examples.

To my friends that have supported me every step of the way. These friends in particular have given me inspiration, purpose, knowledge, experience and back-up.

Those at my church that have helped me gain the spiritual freedom that I've dreamed about, the knowledge that I've thirsted for and for helping provide me with the expansive tools I have today: Ron, David, Luis, Rex, Jim, Jesse, Sarah, Mirit, Grant, Kirstie, Elena and many others.

My haters and keyboard warriors. I couldn't have written the properties without the complete motivation I receive through the amount of ignorance that is thrown my way.

To all of my friends, former classmates, former colleagues, former co-workers, former bosses and managers, mentors, investors: Where I'm at right now is because of you and your support.

Thank you. These properties are fully my own work. They don't symbolize any of the religion's beliefs, practices nor do these writings represent the religion in any shape or form. These are my writings based on my research.

Those who would like more information on the Church of Scientology should visit their official website (Scientology.org), read L. Ron Hubbard's books (found online, libraries, bookstores and at their Churches), as he is the Founder and would know what it is, how it was developed, how he researched it all, how to use it and every other detail you could possibly think of.

I appreciate the time you invested into reading this property.

I invite you to my next property, *The Misconception Manual*. This is to be used as a reference to clearing up the misconceptions of the Church of Scientology.

Thank you,

Ryan Prescott
Twitter: @_Ryan_Prescott

GLOSSARY

A&E Network: A&E is an American pay television network, the flagship television property of A&E Networks. It is headquartered in New York City. (Wikipedia)

Advanced Organization (AO): Scientology Advanced Organizations minister advanced services, providing training through Class VIII and auditing through New OT V.

At an Advanced Organization, the individual recovers lost abilities and gains new insights into the nature of his own spirituality, his relationship to others, the material universe and the Eighth Dynamic. Thus it is not surprising to find that an atmosphere of spiritual discovery permeates these Churches. Those who come to an Advanced Organization have studied diligently to reach this point on the Bridge and ascending the OT levels is a significant step. It is here that individuals fully recover true certainty of their own spirituality and become confident of their ability to play and win the game of life—not only today but far into the future.

Affidavit: a written statement confirmed by oath or affirmation, for use as evidence in court. (Oxford)

Allegation: (n) A claim or assertion that someone has done something illegal or wrong, typically one made without proof. (Oxford)

Alley, Kirstie: Scientologist. Kirstie Louise Alley is an American actress and spokesmodel. She first achieved recognition in 1982, playing Saavik in the science fiction film Star Trek II: The

Wrath of Khan. Alley played Rebecca Howe on the NBC sitcom Cheers, receiving an Emmy Award and a Golden Globe in 1991 for the role. (Wikipedia)

Allure: (v) Powerfully attract or charm; tempt.

Alter: (v) Change in character or composition, typically in a comparatively small but significant way. (Oxford)

Anti-Scientology Cult (ASC): A small and corrupt group of individuals united for the purpose of attacking Scientology. Their mission is to attack the Church of Scientology for publicity and money. These individuals are to project what they're doing onto the Church of Scientology and Scientologists.

Apostate: (n) a person who abandons his or her religion, party, cause, etc Word origin: ME apostate, apostata < OFr apostate & ML apostata < LL(Ec) apostata < Gr(Ec) apostates < Gr, deserter, rebel: see apostasy (Collins English Dictionary)

Applied Scholastics: Applied Scholastics is a nonprofit, public benefit corporation dedicated to improving education with L. Ron Hubbard's learning and literacy tools, collectively known as Study Technology.

Aptitude Test: (n) A test designed to determine a person's ability in a particular skill or field of knowledge. (Oxford)

Artifact: (n) An object made by a human being, typically an item of cultural or historical interest. (Oxford)

Auditing (Pastoral Counseling): Auditing, from the Latin audire meaning "to hear or listen", is the name given to a range of Scientology procedures intended to help people become aware of their spiritual nature and more able in life. Auditing can be ministered to a group (such as at a Scientology Sunday service) or to an individual on a one-to-one basis. A person can also minister certain auditing to himself. All Scientology churches have rooms designated for auditing. (Church of Scientology International)

Auditor: Auditor is defined as one who listens, from the Latin audire meaning to hear or listen. An auditor is a minister or minister-in-training of the Church of Scientology. (Church of Scientology International)

Blackmail: (n) The action, treated as a criminal offense, of demanding payment or another benefit from someone in return for not revealing compromising or damaging information about them. (Oxford)

Bridge, the: the route to Clear and OT, also referred to as the Bridge to Total Freedom. In Scientology there is the idea of a bridge across the chasm. It comes from an old mystic idea of a chasm between where one is now and a higher plateau of existence and that many people trying to make it fell into the abyss. Today, however, Scientology has a bridge that goes across the chasm and is complete and can be walked. It is represented in the steps of the Grade Chart.

Case(s): 1. A general term for a person about to be audited or being audited. 2. All the content of the reactive mind.

Case gain: the improvements and resurgences a person experiences from auditing. Also, any case betterment according to the pc.

Case Supervisor: an accomplished and properly certified auditor who is trained additionally to supervise cases. The C/S is the auditor's "handler". He tells the auditor what to do, corrects his tech, keeps the line straight and keeps the auditor calm and willing and winning. The C/S is the pc's case director.

Censorship: (n) The suppression or prohibition of any parts of books, films, news, etc. that are considered obscene, politically unacceptable, or a threat to security. (Oxford)

Christensen, Erika: Scientologist. Erika Jane Christensen is an American actress and singer whose filmography includes roles in Traffic, Swimfan, The Banger Sisters, The Perfect Score, Flightplan, How to Rob a Bank, The Tortured, and The Case for Christ.

Church of Scientology International (CSI): Church of Scientology International (CSI), the mother church of the Scientology religion, is headquartered in Los Angeles, California. CSI oversees the ecclesiastical activities of all Scientology Churches, organizations and groups world over and ensures that individual Churches receive guidance in their ministries. CSI also provides the broad planning and direction needed to support the Church's international growth.

Church of Spiritual Technology (CST): Church of Spiritual Technology (CST) is a California nonprofit religious corporation formed in 1982 to preserve and archive the Scientology scripture and so ensure its availability for all future generations. It is a Church in the Scientology religion.

Citizens Commission on Human Rights (CCHR): The Citizens Commission on Human Rights (CCHR) was formed by the Church of Scientology and psychiatrist-author Thomas Szasz in 1969. It works to expose psychiatric violations of human rights and clean up the field of mental healing.

Clear: Clear is the name of a state achieved through auditing and describes a being who no longer has his own reactive mind, the hidden source of irrational behavior, unreasonable fears, upsets and insecurities. Without a reactive mind, individuals regain their basic personality, self-determinism and, in essence, become much, much more themselves.

Confessional: a procedure in Scientology whereby an individual is able to confess his withholds and the overt acts underlying them as the first step toward taking responsibility for them and seeking to make things right again.

Conspiracy Theory: (n) A belief that some covert but influential organization is responsible for an unexplained event.

Controversy: (n) Prolonged public disagreement or heated discussion.

Course Supervisor: the person in charge of a Dianetics or Scientology course who is responsible for the training of students and graduating auditors and other graduates at a high level of technology.

Creepy-Crawly: (n) A spider, worm, or other small flightless creature, especially when considered unpleasant or frightening.

Criminon: Criminon, meaning "no crime," is a volunteer criminal rehabilitation program which utilizes technologies developed by L. Ron Hubbard to help convicts recover pride and self-esteem.

Cruise, Tom: Scientologist. Thomas Cruise is an American actor and film producer. He has received several accolades for his work, including three Golden Globe Awards and nominations for three Academy Awards. (Wikipedia)

Crusade: (n) A vigorous campaign for political, social, or religious change.

Cult: (n) A relatively small group of people having religious beliefs or practices regarded by others as strange or as imposing excessive control over members. Early 17th century (originally denoting homage paid to a divinity): from French culte or Latin cultus 'worship', from cult- 'inhabited, cultivated, worshiped', from the verb colere. (Oxford)

Dandar, Ken: Lawyer. Based in Florida, Dandar is on call for anything Anti-Scientology. He's known for money laundering (based on the Lisa McPherson Trust affidavits by Robert Minton), coercing the witnesses to lie under oath, paying witnesses to testify, and he is well-respected by the Anti-Scientology Cult members.

Defamation: (n) The action of damaging the good reputation of someone; slander or libel. (Oxford)

Deflect: (v) Cause (someone) to deviate from an intended purpose.

Defray: (v) Provide money to pay (a cost or expense)

Degrade: (v) Lower the character or quality of.

Deposition: (n) A formal, usually written, statement to be used as evidence. (Oxford)

Deprogram: (v) Release (someone) from apparent brainwashing, typically that of a religious cult, by the systematic re-indoctrination of conventional values. (Oxford)

Despicable: (adj.) Deserving hatred and contempt.

Dianetics: The word Dianetics is derived from the Greek dia, meaning "through," and nous, "mind or soul." Dianetics is further defined as "what the soul is doing to the body." When the mind adversely affects the body, it is described as a psychosomatic condition. Psycho refers to "mind or soul" and somatic refers to "body." Thus, psychosomatic illnesses are physical illnesses caused by the soul.

L. Ron Hubbard discovered the single source of nightmares, unreasonable fears, upsets, insecurities and psychosomatic illness —the reactive mind. In his book Dianetics: The Modern Science of Mental Health he described the reactive mind in detail and laid out a simple, practical, easily taught technology to overcome it and reach the state of Clear. Dianetics is that technology.

Disgruntled: (adj.) Angry or dissatisfied (Oxford)

Distilled: (adj.) Having been shortened so that only the essential meaning or most important aspects remain.

E-Meter: E-Meter is a shortened term for electropsychometer. It is a religious artifact used as a spiritual guide in auditing. It is for use only by a Scientology minister or a Scientology minister-in-training to help the preclear locate and confront areas of spiritual upset.

Ecclesiastical: (adj.) of or relating to a church, especially as an established institution (Merriam-Webster)

Epitomize: (v) Be a perfect example of.

Enterbulation: agitation or disturbance; commotion and upset.

Entheta: a compound word meaning enterbulated theta, theta in a turbulent state, agitated or disturbed. (Theta is the energy of thought and life. Theta is reason, serenity, stability, happiness, cheerful emotion, persistence and the other factors which Man ordinarily considers desirable. The complete description of theta is contained in Science of Survival.)

Ethics Officer(s): the person in a Scientology organization who has the following purpose: To help Ron clear organizations and the public if need be of entheta and enterbulation so that Scientology can be done.

Expose: (v) Make (something) visible by uncovering it. (Oxford)

Exteriorization: Exteriorization is the state of the thetan, the individual himself, being outside the body with or without full perception, but still able to control and handle the body.

Fair Game: A policy written by L. Ron Hubbard and cancelled in 1968 based on misconceptions, misinterpretations, and misapplications. This policy meant that any Scientologists being attacked by a Suppressive Person may take this outside of the Scientology Ethics System and directly to a Court of Law. This is used today, incorrectly, by the Anti-Scientology Cult members to attack the Church in litigation with lawyers like Gerry Armstrong and Ken Dandar. This policy has been rewritten by the Anti-Scientologists and is being used by those wanting to ruthlessly attack Scientology.

fall prey to (also be or become prey to): Be vulnerable to or overcome by. (Oxford)

Field Staff Members (FSM): Field staff members are individual Scientologists who disseminate Scientology and help raise funds for the Church by providing basic Scientology books to interested friends, family members and acquaintances, and introducing other interested individuals to the Church. Field staff members are appointed by their nearest Scientology Church. Because they have had immense spiritual gains from Dianetics and Scientology, field staff members naturally want to share the technology with others.

Flabbergast: (v) Surprise (someone) greatly; astonish. (Oxford)

Flag Service Organization (Flag): Flag (the Flag Service Organization) is a religious retreat located in Clearwater, Florida. It serves as the spiritual headquarters for Scientologists planetwide. Flag is the largest Church of Scientology in the world. Flag represents the hub of the greater Scientology worldwide community as a dynamic, multilingual organization. Flag not only ministers the most advanced levels of training available anywhere, but all advanced levels of auditing up to New OT VII.

The title "Flag" follows from the fact that from the late 1960s through the mid-1970s, the highest ecclesiastical organizations were located at sea aboard a flotilla of ships. The 330-foot motor vessel Apollo served as Mr. Hubbard's home. Accordingly, it was then the most senior Scientology Church. It was known as the "Flagship" of the flotilla and called "Flag" for short.

Foundation for a Drug-Free World: The Foundation for a Drug-Free World is a nonprofit organization headquartered in Los Angeles, California, and dedicated to the eradication of illicit drugs, their abuse and their attendant criminality.

Freewinds (FSSO): The motor vessel Freewinds is a 440-foot ship based in the Caribbean. Its home port is Curacao. The ship, in turn, is the home of the Flag Ship Service Organization (FSSO), a religious retreat ministering the most advanced level of spiritual counseling in the Scientology religion.

The Freewinds provides a safe, aesthetic, distraction-free environment appropriate for ministration of this profoundly spiritual level of auditing. Thus, while the Flag Service Organization in Clearwater ministers the highest levels of training and auditing from the bottom of the Bridge to New OT VII, the most advanced OT level (New OT VIII) is exclusively entrusted to the

FSSO.

Golden Era Productions: Set on 500 acres in Southern California, this is the worldwide dissemination center for the entire Scientology religion, responsible for all film, video, television, Internet and international event production.

HGC: abbreviation for Hubbard Guidance Center, the Department of Processing in a Church of Scientology organization where auditing is delivered to preclears.

Ideal: (adj.) Satisfying one's conception of what is perfect; most suitable. (Oxford)

Immunity: (n) Protection or exemption from something, especially an obligation or penalty. (Oxford)

Impression: (n) An idea, feeling, or opinion about something or someone, especially one formed without conscious thought or on the basis of little evidence. (Oxford)

Inaugurate: (v) Mark the beginning or first public use of (an organization or project) with a special event or ceremony. (Oxford)

Inextricably: (adverb) In a way that is impossible to disentangle or separate. (Oxford)

Infiltrate: (v) Enter or gain access to (an organization, place, etc.) surreptitiously and gradually, especially in order to acquire secret information. (Oxford)

Innuendo: (n) An allusive or oblique remark or hint, typically a suggestive or disparaging one. (Oxford)

Internal Revenue: Revenue derived from duties and taxes imposed on domestic trade and commerce; inland revenue; (also, often with capital initials) an agency responsible for collecting this; frequently attributive, especially in "Internal Revenue Service". (Oxford)

International Association of Scientologists (IAS): The International Association of Scientologists (IAS) is an unincorporated membership organization open to all Scientologists from all nations.

International Hubbard Ecclesiastical League of Pastors (I HELP): The International Hubbard Ecclesiastical League of Pastors (I HELP) was created to provide assistance to auditors who minister religious services in the field and thus outside organized Churches.

International Justice Chief: the executive in Senior HCO International responsible for the standard application of Scientology Justice policies to staff and public. He is a protector of the Church and its tenets and membership. His duties include reviewing and approving (or not approving) any major justice actions to ensure that no injustice is done. He is assisted by Continental Justice Chiefs in each Continental Senior HCO.

Introspection Rundown: an auditing rundown which helps a preclear locate and correct those things which cause him to have his attention inwardly fixated. He then becomes capable of looking outward so he can see his environment, handle and control it.

Liberation: (n) Freedom from limits on thought or behavior. (Oxford)

Lobotomy: (n) A surgical operation involving incision into the prefrontal lobe of the brain, formerly used to treat mental illness. (Oxford)

LRH: Initials of L. Ron Hubbard, Founder of Scientology and Dianetics

Masterson, Danny: Scientologist. Daniel Peter Masterson is an American actor and disc jockey. Masterson played the roles of Steven Hyde in That '70s Show and Jameson "Rooster" Bennett in The Ranch. (Wikipedia)

Minton, Robert: Investor. Sponsored witch hunts against Scientology in Clearwater, FL, one Anti-Scientology film, interviewed on multiple talk shows, and lost over $7,000,000 after being conned by members of the Anti-Scientology Cult. One of the investors of the Lisa McPherson Trust and exposed it from the inside with two scathing affidavits against Anti-Scientologists and corrupt lawyer, Ken Dandar.

Miscavige, David: David Miscavige is the ecclesiastical leader of the Scientology religion. From his position as Chairman of the Board of Religious Technology Center (RTC), Mr. Miscavige bears the ultimate responsibility for ensuring the standard and pure application of L. Ron Hubbard's technologies of Dianetics and Scientology and for Keeping Scientology Working. (Scientology)

Moderator: (n) An arbitrator or mediator. (Oxford)

motivator(s): acts received by the person or individual causing injury, reduction or degradation of his beingness, person, associations or dynamics. A motivator is called a "motivator" because it tends to prompt an overt. When a person commits an overt or overt of omission with no motivator, he tends to believe or pretends that he has received a motivator which does not in fact exist. This is a *false motivator*. Beings suffering from this are said to have "motivator hunger" and are often aggrieved over nothing.

Narconon: Narconon is a highly effective drug-free withdrawal, detoxification and rehabilitation program which utilizes techniques developed by L. Ron Hubbard. Narconon, meaning "no drugs," began as a grass-roots movement in the mid-1960s when an inmate of the Arizona State Prison solved his own drug problem using principles found in one of L. Ron Hubbard's books. He then used those same principles to help solve drug-related problems of fellow inmates.

Narrative: (n) A spoken or written account of connected events; a story.

Non-Profit: (adj.) Not making or conducted primarily to make a profit. (Oxford)

of (or by or on) one's own volition: (n) Voluntarily.

Ortega, Tony: Anti-Religious Blogger. Once hired by the Village Voice, wrote over 100 conspiracy theories against the Church of Scientology, fired due to his connection with Backpage (the prostitution sex ring online) and Village Voice's ties, he was paid off. Anti-Scientology Cult member and Propagandist.

OT: Operating Thetan (OT) is a spiritual state of being above Clear. By Operating is meant "able to act and handle things" and by Thetan is meant "the spiritual being that is the basic self." An Operating Thetan, then, is one who can handle things without having to use a body of physical means.

OT Levels (sections, courses, etc.): the advanced Scientology training and auditing actions that enable a Clear to reach the state of Operating Thetan.
Overt: a harmful act or a transgression against the moral code of a group is called an "overt act" or an "overt". When a person does something that is contrary to the moral code he has agreed to, or when he omits to do something that he should have done per that moral code, he has committed an overt act. An overt act violates what was agreed upon. It is an act by the person or individual leading to the injury, reduction or degradation of another, others or their beingness, persons, possessions, associations or dynamics. It can be intentional or unintentional.

Out-ethics: an action or situation in which an individual is involved, or something the individual does, which is contrary to the ideals, best interests and survival of his dynamics.

Overt of omission: a failure to act resulting in the injury, reduction or degradation of another or others or their beingness, persons, possessions or dynamics.

Oxford Capacity Analysis (Personality Test): The Oxford Capacity Analysis (OCA) is a self-report test utilized in Scientology Churches since the 1950s to measure changes in how people feel about themselves. People may complete an OCA through the mail or in the Test Center of a Church of Scientology.

Perjury: (n) The offense of willfully telling an untruth or making a misrepresentation under oath. (Oxford)

Philosophy: (n) The study of the fundamental nature of knowledge, reality, and existence, especially when considered as an academic discipline.

Postulate: (v) Suggest or assume the existence, fact, or truth of (something) as a basis for reasoning, discussion, or belief. (Oxford)

Potential Trouble Source (PTS): somebody who is connected with a Suppressive Person who is invalidating him, his beingness, his life. The person is a Potential Trouble Source because he is connected to the Suppressive Person. Potential Trouble Source means the person is going to go up and fall down. And he is a trouble source because he is going to get upset and because he is going to make trouble. And he really does make trouble. That's very carefully named.

Preclear: A person receiving auditing is called a preclear—from pre (before) and "Clear," a person not yet Clear. A preclear is a person who, through auditing, is finding out more about himself and life.

Preston, Kelly: Scientologist. Kelly Kamalelehua Smith, better known by her stage name Kelly Preston, is an American actress and former model. She has appeared in more than sixty television and film productions, most notably including Mischief, Twins, and Jerry Maguire.

Projection: (n) The unconscious transfer of one's desires or emotions to another person. (Oxford)

Public Relations: (p. n) The professional maintenance of a favorable public image by a company or other organization or a famous person. (Oxford)

Purification Rundown: The Purification Rundown is a detoxification program which enables an individual to rid himself of the harmful effects of drugs, toxins and other chemicals that lodge in the body and create a biochemical barrier to spiritual well-being.

Reactive mind: that portion of a person's mind which works on a totally stimulus-response basis (given a certain stimulus it gives a certain response), which is not under his volitional control, and which exerts force and the power of command over his awareness, purposes, thoughts, body and actions.

Rehabilitation Project Force (RPF): The Rehabilitation Project Force (RPF) is a religious program undertaken by a very small number of members of the Church of Scientology. Neither staff members who work in local Churches of Scientology around the world nor Church parishioners would qualify to undertake this program. Only those who belong to the religious order of the Church of Scientology, the Sea Organization, may do the RPF, and then only for specific reasons. The purpose of the RPF is to provide a "second chance" to those who have failed to fulfill their ecclesiastical responsibilities as members of the Sea Organization.

The Rehabilitation Project Force is a voluntary program of spiritual rehabilitation. The emphasis is on the word "rehabilitation," meaning, in this context, to restore one's condition to an optimal spiritual state. It represents a free religious commitment by the individual to a spiritual discipline. The word "force" in this context means "[A] group of people working or acting together." (Thorndike Barnhart Dictionary, 1992)

Religion: (n) A particular system of faith and worship. Middle English (originally in the sense 'life under monastic vows'): from Old French, from Latin religio(n-) 'obligation, bond, reverence', perhaps based on Latin religare 'to bind'. (Oxford)

Religious Technology Center (RTC): Religious Technology Center (RTC) is a nonprofit religious organization formed in 1982 to preserve, maintain and protect the Scientology religion and is a Church of the Scientology religion.

Remini, Leah: Apostate of the Church of Scientology. Expelled. Extortionist, family separator, failed at meeting the ethical standards of an average Scientologist, and Anti-Scientology Cult Leader.

Ribisi, Giovanni: Scientologist. Antonino Giovanni Ribisi, known professionally as Giovanni Ribisi, is an American film and television actor known for his roles in Avatar and Ted and the TV series Sneaky Pete. He also had recurring roles in My Name Is Earl and Friends.

Rinder, Mike: Apostate of the Church of Scientology. Expelled. Wife beater, suborner of perjury, admitted liar, and Anti-Scientology Cult member. Formerly the temporary International Spokesperson for the Church of Scientology International before demoted due to abandonment, unproductivity, and lying to the chain of command.

Sacrosanct: (adj.) (especially of a principle, place, or routine) regarded as too important or valuable to be interfered with. (Oxford)

Saint Hill: Saint Hill Churches are the next level above Class V Churches.

The original Saint Hill Church is located in East Grinstead, Sussex, England, where Mr. Hubbard resided from 1959 to 1966. At Saint Hill, Mr. Hubbard made some of his most significant discoveries on the mind and spirit and regularly released these discoveries in daily lectures attended by advanced students of Scientology from around the world. Today, this body of Scientology scripture, known as the Saint Hill Special Briefing Course, is the most extensive auditor training course in Scientology and comprises nearly 450 recorded lectures and other written materials. These Churches also minister some of the most advanced levels of auditing.

Scientologist: (n) A member of the Church of Scientology.

Scientology: Scientology, conceived by L. Ron Hubbard, comes from the Latin scio which means "knowing, in the fullest meaning of the word" and the Greek word logos which means "study of." It means knowing how to know. Scientology is further defined as "the study and handling of the spirit in relationship to itself, universes and other life." (Church of Scientology International)

Scientology Missions (Missions): Scientology Missions reach out into their communities to provide help where most needed and to bring new people into contact with Scientology and encourage their spiritual advancement through the higher levels of the religion. Missions minister basic Scientology religious services including the lower levels of auditing and introductory training.

Scientology Volunteer Minister (VM): Founded by L. Ron Hubbard in the early 1970s, the Volunteer Minister program was designed to provide practical Scientology tools and indiscriminate help in an often cynical and cruel world.

Scobee, Amy: Apostate of the Church of Scientology. Expelled. Admitted liar, caught sleeping with those she was counseling, dismissed from over 10 positions, couldn't meet the ethical standards of an average Scientologist, and Anti-Scientology Cult member.

Sea Organization, The (Sea Org): The Sea Organization is a religious order for the Scientology religion and is composed of the singularly most dedicated Scientologists—individuals who have committed their lives to the volunteer service of their religion. The Sea Organization is a fraternal religious order and is not incorporated. Members of the Sea Organization are therefore wholly responsible to the Church of Scientology to which they are assigned and are responsible, as are all other staff, to officers and directors of that Church.

Sheer: (adj.) Nothing other than; unmitigated (used for emphasis) (Oxford)

Slander: (n) The action or crime of making a false spoken statement damaging to a person's reputation. (Oxford)

Sleazy: (adj.) (of a person or situation) sordid, corrupt, or immoral. (Oxford)

Sound Bite: (n) A short extract from a recorded interview or speech, chosen for its succinctness or concision. (Oxford)

Study Tech: the term given to the methods developed by L. Ron Hubbard that enable individuals to study effectively. It is an exact technology that anyone can use to learn a subject or to acquire a new skill. It provides an understanding of the fundamental principles of how to learn and gives precise ways to overcome the barriers and pitfalls one can encounter during study such as going by misunderstood words or symbols.

Suppressive Person (SP): A Suppressive Person (SP) is a person who seeks to suppress other people in their vicinity. A Suppressive Person will goof up or vilify any effort to help anybody and particularly knife with violence anything calculated to make human beings more powerful or more intelligent.

Szasz, Dr. Thomas: American psychiatrist, university professor and writer, well known for his highly critical views of the practices of psychiatry. Szasz has written over 200 articles and several books.

Technology (tech): the methods of application of an art or science as opposed to mere knowledge of the science or art itself. In Scientology, the term technology refers to the methods of application of Scientology principles to improve the functions of the mind and rehabilitate the potentials of the spirit, developed by L. Ron Hubbard.

Thetan(s): the person himself - not his body or his name, the physical universe, his mind, or anything else; that which is aware of being aware; the identity which is the individual.

The Way to Happiness (TWTH): L. Ron Hubbard's The Way to Happiness is a common sense guide to better living comprised of 21 precepts, each predicated on the fact that survival is interdependent and without universal brotherhood there is no joy and there is no happiness.

Transgress: (v) Go beyond the limits of (what is morally, socially, or legally acceptable) (Oxford)

Travolta, John: Scientologist. John Joseph Travolta is an American singer, actor, and dancer. Travolta rose to fame during the

1970s, appearing on the television series Welcome Back, Kotter and starring in the box office successes Saturday Night Fever and Grease. (Wikipedia)

Unadulterated: (adj.) Not mixed or diluted with any different or extra elements; complete and absolute. (Oxford)

Unincorporated: (adj.) (of a company or other organization) not formed into a legal corporation.

Usher: (v) Cause or mark the start of something new.

Withhold: an unspoken, unannounced transgression against a moral code by which the person is bound is called a "withhold". A withhold is an overt act that a person committed that he or she is not talking about. It is something a person believes that if revealed will endanger his self-preservation. Any withhold comes after an overt.

Youth for Human Rights: Youth for Human Rights International (YHRI) is a nonprofit organization founded in 2001 by Dr. Mary Shuttleworth, an educator born and raised in apartheid South Africa, where she witnessed firsthand the devastating effects of discrimination and the lack of basic human rights.

REFERENCES

"Total Fraud", Leah Remini Aftermath 2018, Church of Scientology International, July 5, 2019, https://www.leahreminiaftermath.com/articles/total-fraud.html

"Letter from CSI to Weresow of 23 November 2016 re The Practice of "Disconnection", Leah Remini Aftermath, November 23, 2016, Church of Scientology International, July 1, 2019, https://www.leahreminiaftermath.com/letters/20161123-csi-to-weresow-re-practice-of-disconnection.html#

Mark Rathbun. "Rinder on Narconon." YouTube, 5 Feb. 2018, https://www.youtube.com/watch?v=AB5XTkBQPWM.

Mark Rathbun. "Anti-Scientology Cult Censorship." YouTube, 5 Feb. 2018, https://www.youtube.com/watch?v=c6ApWHsWaj8.

Mark Rathbun. "Scientology Tax Exemption" YouTube, 5 Feb. 2018, https://www.youtube.com/watch?v=wVxeDjgjKpc

Mark Rathbun. "Remini's Rinder: Scientology Helps" YouTube, 5 Feb. 2018, https://www.youtube.com/watch?v=MO8OsuFLpXg

Mark Rathbun. "Ventriloquist Dummies" YouTube, 5 Feb. 2018, https://www.youtube.com/watch?v=MiOYTyBLqG8

Mark Rathbun. "Anti-Scientology Vanityland" YouTube, 5 Feb. 2018, https://www.youtube.com/watch?v=vUxLjkZVzJI

Mark Rathbun. "Anti-Scientologist Rationalization" YouTube, 5 Feb. 2018, https://www.youtube.com/watch?v=U1ulSfcV-qw

Mark Rathbun. "Remini's Reality TV Acting" YouTube, 5 Feb. 2018, https://youtu.be/MjbiYwU2MEs

Mark Rathbun. "Snow White" YouTube, 5 Feb. 2018, https://www.youtube.com/watch?v=bnhLgRbCikY

Mark Rathbun. "Anti-Scientology Passive-aggressive Treatment" YouTube, 5 Feb. 2018, https://www.youtube.com/watch?v=IHlFm6To2M4&t=47s

Mark Rathbun. "Anti-Scientology Passive-aggressive Treatment" YouTube, 5 Feb. 2018,
https://youtu.be/IHlFm6To2M4

Mark Rathbun. "Backpage Tony Ortega" YouTube, 5 Feb. 2018,
https://youtu.be/MspGkPZJ7l8
Mark Rathbun. "Paul Haggis Hypocrisy" YouTube, 5 Feb. 2018,
https://youtu.be/JLrqfxHSC2g

Mark Rathbun. "Leah Remini and her Troublemakers" YouTube, 22 Jun. 2017,
https://youtu.be/9_JcoOh1dBg

Mark Rathbun. "Leah Remini and her Troublemakers, Part 2" YouTube, 22 Jun. 2017,
https://youtu.be/SasJoQKUw_k

Mark Rathbun. "Leah Remini and her Troublemakers, Part 3" YouTube, 22 Jun. 2017,
https://youtu.be/8vfSazTH8is

Mark Rathbun. "Leah Remini and her Troublemakers, Part 4" YouTube, 23 Jun. 2017,
https://youtu.be/Yp8tyANTkpc

Mark Rathbun. "Leah Remini and her Troublemakers, Part 5" YouTube, 24 Jun. 2017,
https://youtu.be/mj-MRBhbmzA

Mark Rathbun. "Leah Remini and her Troublemakers, Part 6" YouTube, 25 Jun. 2017,
https://youtu.be/k1fj3WRCrzo

Mark Rathbun. "Going Clear, Part 5" YouTube, 11 Jun. 2017,
https://youtu.be/B8MoZLfJa9s

Mark Rathbun. "Going Clear, Part 1" YouTube, 7 Jun. 2017,
https://youtu.be/aFwCysSCw4g

Mark Rathbun. "INTRO" YouTube, 6 Jun. 2017,
https://youtu.be/ZFJdOhV29WM

"Total Fraud", Leah Remini Aftermath 2018, Church of Scientology International, July 5, 2019, https://www.leahreminiaftermath.com/articles/total-fraud.html

"Bigotry and Hate Exposed: Mike Rinder" STAND League 2015-2019, Scientologists Taking Action Against Discrimination, June 8, 2019
https://www.standleague.org/bigotry-and-hate/exposed/mike-rinder.html#

"Mike Rinder testimony in 1994" STAND League 2015-2019, Scientologists Taking Action Against Discrimination, June 8, 2019 https://www.standleague.org/bigotry-and-hate/exposed/mike-rinder/rinder-testimony-1994.html#

"Trespass citation on Mike Rinder" STAND League 2015-2019, Scientologists Taking Action Against Discrimination, June 9, 2019 https://www.standleague.org/bigotry-and-hate/exposed/mike-rinder/trespass-citation.html#

"Mike Rinder deposition on January 6, 2015" STAND League 2015-2019, Scientologists Taking Action Against Discrimination, June 11, 2019 https://www.standleague.org/bigotry-and-hate/exposed/mike-rinder/rinder-deposition-2015.html#

"Medical report re injuries by Mike Rinder" STAND League 2015-2019, Scientologists Taking Action Against Discrimination, June 12, 2019 https://www.standleague.org/bigotry-and-hate/exposed/mike-rinder/documented-injuries.html#

"The "Scientology Aftermath" Video Leah Remini Tried to Suppress", Leah Remini Aftermath, 2017-2019, Church of Scientology International, July 2, 2019, https://www.leahreminiaftermath.com/articles/the-scientology-aftermath-video-leah-remini-tried-to-suppress.html#

"What is Disconnection?", Scientology Attitudes and Practices, 2019, Church of Scientology International, May 2, 2019, https://www.scientology.org/faq/scientology-attitudes-and-practices/what-is-disconnection.html

"DID L. RON HUBBARD MAKE A LOT OF MONEY OUT OF SCIENTOLOGY?", Scientology Founder, 2019, Church of Scientology International, May 2, 2019, https://www.scientology.org/faq/scientology-founder/did-l-ron-hubbard-make-a-lot-of-money-out-of-scientology.html

"WHAT WAS L. RON HUBBARD'S ROLE IN THE CHURCH?", Scientology Founder, 2019, Church of Scientology International, May 2, 2019, https://www.scientology.org/faq/scientology-founder/what-was-l-ron-hubbards-role-in-the-church.html

"DO SCIENTOLOGISTS BELIEVE THAT L. RON HUBBARD WAS LIKE JESUS CHRIST?", Scientology Founder, 2019, Church of Scientology International, May 2, 2019, https://www.scientology.org/faq/scientology-founder/do-scientologists-believe-that-l-ron-hubbard-was-like-jesus-christ.html

"HOW ARE CHURCHES OF SCIENTOLOGY SUPPORTED FINANCIALLY?", Church Funding, 2019, Church of Scientology International, May 4, 2019, https://www.scientology.org/faq/church-funding/church-funding.html

"WHAT IS THE SIGNIFICANCE OF THE IRS RULING REGARDING CHURCHES OF SCIENTOLOGY?", Church Funding, 2019, Church of Scientology International, May 5, 2019, https://www.scientology.org/faq/church-funding/significance-of-irs-ruling.html

"WHAT IS THE INTERNATIONAL ASSOCIATION OF SCIENTOLOGISTS?", Church Funding, 2019, Church of Scientology International, May 5, 2019, https://www.scientology.org/faq/scientology-in-society/what-is-the-international-association-of-scientologists.html

"WHAT ABOUT THOSE WHO CANNOT AFFORD TO MAKE DONATIONS FOR SERVICES?", Church Funding, 2019, Church of Scientology International, May 7, 2019, https://www.scientology.org/faq/church-funding/what-about-those-without-funds-for-donations.html

"IS THE CHURCH PROFIT-MAKING?", Church Funding, 2019, Church of Scientology International, May 8, 2019, https://www.scientology.org/faq/church-funding/is-the-church-profit-making.html

"WHAT IS THE SEA ORGANIZATION?", Church Management, 2019, Church of Scientology International, May 8, 2019, https://www.scientology.org/faq/church-management/what-is-the-sea-organization.html

"WHAT IS FLAG?", THE ORGANIZATION OF SCIENTOLOGY , 2019, Church of Scientology International, May 9, 2019, https://www.scientology.org/faq/the-organization-of-scientology/what-is-flag.html

"IS SCIENTOLOGY A CULT?", SCIENTOLOGY AND OTHER PRACTICES , 2019, Church of Scientology International, May 10, 2019, https://www.scientology.org/faq/the-organization-of-scientology/what-is-flag.html

"WHAT IS AUDITING?", SCIENTOLOGY AND DIANETICS AUDITING, 2019, Church of Scientology International, May 10, 2019, https://www.scientology.org/faq/scientology-and-dianetics-auditing/what-is-auditing.html

"WHAT IS THE E-METER AND HOW DOES IT WORK?", SCIENTOLOGY AND DIANETICS AUDITING, 2019, Church of Scientology International, May 10, 2019, https://www.scientology.org/faq/scientology-and-dianetics-auditing/what-is-the-emeter-and-how-does-it-work.html

"IS INFORMATION DIVULGED DURING AUDITING SESSIONS ALWAYS KEPT CONFIDENTIAL?", SCIENTOLOGY AND DIANETICS AUDITING, 2019, Church of Scientology International, May 10, 2019, https://www.scientology.org/faq/scientology-and-dianetics-auditing/is-information-divulged-during-auditing-sessions-always-kept-confidential.html

"WHAT DO THE TERMS PRECLEAR AND AUDITOR MEAN?", SCIENTOLOGY

AND DIANETICS AUDITING, 2019, Church of Scientology International, May 10, 2019, https://www.scientology.org/faq/scientology-and-dianetics-auditing/what-do-the-terms-preclear-and-auditor-mean.html

"WHAT WILL I GET OUT OF AUDITING?", SCIENTOLOGY AND DIANETICS AUDITING, 2019, Church of Scientology International, May 10, 2019, https://www.scientology.org/faq/scientology-and-dianetics-auditing/what-will-I-get-out-of-auditing.html

"WHAT CAN AUDITING CURE?", SCIENTOLOGY AND DIANETICS AUDITING, 2019, Church of Scientology International, May 11, 2019, https://www.scientology.org/faq/scientology-and-dianetics-auditing/what-can-auditing-cure.html

"ARE AUDITORS GOVERNED BY A CODE OF CONDUCT?", SCIENTOLOGY AND DIANETICS AUDITING, 2019, Church of Scientology International, May 11, 2019, https://www.scientology.org/faq/scientology-and-dianetics-auditing/code-of-conduct-for-scientology-ministers.html

Made in the USA
Monee, IL
19 March 2020